I0748757

foodnbullshit

Peggy,
To you and for you,
You know much of it; well, this is the rest.
What I didn't say.
What I could not say.
What I don't know how to say.
Without you, there would have been nothing.
I would have been nothing.
I would have been no one.
I love you.
Deeply, madly.

SERVICE NOT INCLUDED

ALEX FENOT

The new guard

The old guard

A tale of two

The calm before the shitstorm

Last order

Dream menu

Kitchen Is Closed

Jukebox

Legal mentions

This book was previously published under the title "In the kitchen, no one will hear you burn."

Publisher: Foodnbullshit
First Edition: 2025
Second Edition: 2026
Legal Deposit: Q1
ISBN: 979-8-9931095-9-6

A few words

Finally.
I have finished it.
Holy shit, it's done.
To be honest, even though it was fun to go back through memory lane, it has been sometimes gruesome and painful to walk that mile. And far from being a walk in the park.
It was a grind.
Because it took me three books to end up with one I could live with.

Let me walk you through it and sum up the first version quickly:
I thought, "I've got experience, so I'll tell my story. Maybe give some advice here and there—like a mentor."
But the moment I started rereading some chapters, and I realize something:
Wait a minute... Me, lecturing, patronizing.
If people close to me read that, they're going to have a good laugh.
And I knew right away it wasn't going to work.
I am writing a book about my path. So, if there's one moment where I really need to be truly honest. Not bullshitting myself and not pretending to be someone else...
It's right here, right now.
Besides, who the hell am I kidding?
I'm the opposite of a role model.
So, I scrapped everything.

Second version:
Ironic, loudmouth, cocky. Serious too.
Way too serious.
I read it again, and I felt something was missing.
The main ingredient: me.
Because facts don't lie. I'm a moron with a weird and questionable sense of humor. All in the second degree. Always.
And my life, it has been a mix of bad decisions, countless mistakes, recklessness, and an inconsistency that borders on genius.
So here I go again; I started over.

And here we are. This version is basically the one that is the most honest list of my failures and my screw-ups. And it captures faithfully the way I look at this world—with a legendary stupidity strapped across my chest like a bandolier. And always, the right (or wrong) word at the right (or wrong) time.
They say you can laugh at everything, but not with everyone.
Bullshit.
For me it stops at "We should laugh at everything. And especially about ourselves.
My path has been funny, sometimes pathetic, full of crashes, and sometimes not very glorious. But I always found a way to laugh through it all.
Sometimes bitterly, sure, but still.

According to Serge Gainsbourg, a famous French singer, "stupidity is just intelligence relaxing."

Well, perfect timing.
I invite you on a dumb, messy, epic journey:
My life, my laughter, my dramas, my scars.
And in the background—the restaurant industry.
Because for the past three decades, dining rooms and kitchens have been my battlefield.
My hell, my lost paradise, and my salvation.

And since we're quoting famous people, Sacha Guitry—a French writer... for the clueless—once said the following:
"If you're going to do something stupid, might as well do it with music."
He was talking about marriage, but it fits this story perfectly.
That's why sometimes, you will hear a song pop into a chapter. And every time you'll see this ♫, it means the moment mattered to me.
I'm not emotionally numb, but I just don't talk much. I keep things inside. And as I've always struggled to express my emotions, words often get stuck.
So, music became my shortcut.
And I found it was the best way to make you understand what was going on inside me at the time.

On a more serious note, why not a clean and classic text? Straightforward and without frills and fluffs.
Because I'm impulsive and instinctive. And for a long time I was a wounded beast. A raw nerve.

And those songs were the only things that kept me anchored to a life I sometimes, when I was younger, thought about cutting short.
But they're not here to speak for me.
They're markers, a legend; those riffs, notes, and voices are glued to precise moments of my life.
Not to quote lyrics or slap on a fake soundtrack.
But music has always been my fuel, my rage, and my crutch. It filled a void, sparked hope, or simply brought me back to a place where I could smile again.
Listening to these songs alongside the story is like stepping into my kitchen, my sleepless nights, and my scars.
In the end, it's me screaming; the tracks just set the scene. An atmosphere, an intensity.
If you feel like it, read it and blast the song, and you'll understand exactly what I felt at the time.
But even without them, the essentials remain:
My voice, my guts,
My mess.

And since this note is an intro, might as well kick off with one that sets the tone. One that throws you right into the right mood and gets you ready for what's coming.
I picked a song that isn't a threat but a promise.
One that says that things are about to get loud.
That there will be no bullshit. That I won't sugarcoat anything.
So, grab your iPhone or your iPad, or go to your vinyl collection if you're old school, and scroll to the letter W.

We start with ♫ *Whole Lotta Love* by Led Zeppelin.

Crank it up.
Pedal to the floor.
Shit is going to hit the fan.

On the menu

I've always had this fantasy of making an entrance with a soundtrack—at school, in a restaurant, in my kitchen, at home, even on the damn toilet. Obviously, this chapter had to start with a riff. But not just any riff.

Darth Vader's got his theme;
James Bond as well.
Why the hell not me?

So I'm crashing in with ♫ *Jumpin' Jack Flash,*
by the Rolling Stones.
Because right from the first line, Jagger screams his birth and his existence like some kind of curse.
A bit like me.
This track hits you like boiling sauce exploding straight in your face; it shakes you up.
It's a musical storm that doesn't announce anything good. And by the time Richards plays his guitar, it's already too late.
You're hooked.
This song is pure energy. Raw adrenaline. The kind that kicks you in the ass when you've had three hours of sleep and too much reality.
It's loud, not subtle, and it stains.
It rocks and it rolls.
And it fits perfectly because this book starts with a bang.
Like a fucking Saturday night service
Like a greasy riff from the Stones.

So, here, you'll run into a whole gang of maniacs and lunatics:
Line cooks on the edge of collapse and burned-out servers.
Grumpy chefs and heroic sous-chefs.
Cokeheads and pain-in-the-ass customers.
Friends, glorious idiots, and random ghosts passing through.
Lovable assholes and pathetic losers.
Shitty services and moments of grace.
Gods dressed in white.
A kamikaze in high heels, and even a goddamn dog that knows more about love and loyalty than most people.
And everything that follows isn't just my career in restaurants; it's the tale of a life anything but ordinary. An epic journey stretched across both sides of the Atlantic. And a sharp, ironic, and slightly sarcastic chronicle about a world I no longer fully understand anymore.

So, for those who know me, if you still had questions, this might answer a few.
For everyone else, we don't know each other, and honestly, it's for the best.
Believe me.
So, think of it as a blind date on paper.
But here it's more like a headbutt than love at first sight.
Listen, I know this book won't please everyone.
It won't be a bestseller.
It won't be a critics' darling.

And I couldn't care less.
Yes, it's trashy. It's blunt, and sometimes rude.
You might feel it like a punch in the stomach.
But it's who I am and the way I speak.
The way we speak.
You think when we talk in the kitchen, we send each other love letters with heart emojis as punctuation?
We don't.
I'm a chef. We are cooks, not diplomats.

So, if you're here, either you're a masochist or you've got questionable taste for chaos. Or maybe it's just the cover or the title that snagged your curiosity.
Either way, let's keep it civil for now.
Because it won't last.
So, enjoy it while you can.
In the meantime,
Welcome.
What you're about to read is neither a "feel-good" guide nor a culinary love letter. And not some half-assed polished "success story" wrapped in marketing bullshit.
And let's be honest about me:
I don't hang out in juice bars.
I don't have tattoos.
I'm not politically correct.
I'm not a bearded hipster on an electric scooter.
And finally, quinoa, kale, and tofu make me gag.
On the bright side, I do like teasing people.
So, everyone is going to be roasted, including yours truly.

My three favorite tools: my kitchen knives, my guitars, and trash talking. I use all three every day with depraved joy, enthusiasm, and absolutely no shame whatsoever.
But before I pull them out, let me say this:
Dear customers and readers,
I love you all.
Every single one of you.
Even vegans—don't worry, I'll deal with you later.
Fair and square, like everyone else.
But it's a particular kind of love.
A rough one.
The kind that doesn't always brush you the right way but never lies.

If you're sensitive and already uncomfortable with my tone, it's not going to get easier.
Because this only goes one way: louder and rougher. I'm not here to rock you to sleep; I'm here to give you an electroshock.
And along the way, you will probably disagree with some of the things you're going to read here.
Others may even offend you; I'm sure at least a couple will.
As we say in the industry,
"Management reserves the right to serve."
Well, here it is the same.
The author will reserve the right not to give a flying fuck.
Because at my age and with what I've been through, I've learned to do without other people's approval or opinion.

But if you're curious, if you can handle a bit of roughness, a lot of second-degree humor...
Then we can walk a bit of this road together.

Alright, enough with the romance and the Vaseline.
Let's sit down at the table.
The bartender is going to take your order.
Have a drink before I give you the menu.

Special of the day

Everything that you're about to read isn't even half of what I lived through. I picked out pieces. Moments, samples, here and there.
Unlike what Keith Richards wrote in his autobiography, I don't remember everything. There are some things I do, some I don't, and others I'd rather not.
But even though I could have said ten times more, it wouldn't have changed a thing. The chaos stays the same: messy, dark, and brutal.
I didn't write to tell everything, to be liked, or to come off as a nice guy. I don't give a rat's ass about that.
I wrote to make you feel.
I wrote it because I was smoldering, and if I didn't put out that fire inside, I'd be the one to go up in smoke.
So, take these fragments as they come: raw, imperfect, brutal, but real.

Being a chcf gave me everything.
I found intensity, pride, the beauty of a craft, and passion.
But it cost me plenty in return.
It ruined my health, my sleep, my weekends, and my family life.
A resurrection... maybe.
Somehow.
But at what cost?

Today chefs are everywhere:
On screens, in TV shows, and in filtered social media posts.
But no one talks about kitchens, hardly ever.
The real ones.
The ones that scream, sweat, bleed, and thrive in chaos.
Where cooks wake up at six a.m. and go to bed at two a.m. And do it all over again the next day, broken, exhausted, but still standing.
Lunch and dinner.
Six days a week.
Because we forget, that's right. That's how we're wired. We forget the pain, the absurd hours, the burns, and the pressure.
The epic recipe disasters, the blowups.
The failures. The rage. The chaos.
The customers who think you're their personal chef on demand.
The nights from hell that leave you on your knees.
And yet every day, we put that jacket back on.
Because we love this job in spite of all the shit that comes with it.
It's in our blood.
And that poison...we drink it neat.

I've spent thirty years in the restaurant industry, and for the record, I'm neither a Michelin-star chef nor a fine dining guy.
I never cared about that.
I started in the dining room and ended up in the kitchen. I've left pieces of myself along the way.

Both physical and mental. I've got the brain of a neurotic in the body of a crash test dummy.
I'm a solid chef. Fast. Straightforward. I cook honest and simple meals for people who just want to eat well.
As for my taste in food?
If I have the choice between a three-star tasting menu and some escargots, a juicy rib-eye, a cheese plate, or profiteroles with a decent wine.
Personally, the choice is easy, no contest.
I'll take the local joint, no fluff, no frills, to feast on a paper tablecloth with a checkered napkin and a bottle of wine that enriches the soul.

Now that you know where I stand, think of this book like a raging tribute to a job that gives everything and demands just as much in return.
With interest.
This is a thank-you letter with scars and burns on it.
A testimony of gratitude and spotlight on the people you never see in restaurants.
The cooks who work under flickering neon lights in suffocating heat. Chasing that crooked but honest feeling of a job well done.
The dishwashers, those silent heroes, hidden in the back, hands deep in grease and boiling water.
Commis, no one listens to.
Sous-chefs holding the line without a word.
Chefs, trying to keep the ship afloat while it's sinking.

And the front of the house too.

The servers, who are dealing with increasingly demanding guests and surreal requests. Who run miles every night with trays stacked high, dodging elbows and chairs.
The bartenders, who are standing ten hours straight with their feet soaked in melting ice from a leaking machine.
The hostesses, who are always answering the phone politely, even when you call just to ask if we're open.
If we pick up... what do you think?
In a nutshell, all those who work while others dine.

I wanted a raw style, sharp, with short sentences. A text with a constant tension that reeks of butter, garlic, stress, and rock'n'roll.
Because I write the way I cook: instinctively and always with music.
It's been in my life as far back as I can remember.
Like a noisy companion.
A mirror to my emotions.
When I was young, I hated silence because I couldn't stand hearing my own thoughts.
Now that the rage has passed, I've learned to like it.
The silence between notes.
The silence between the services.

So here, each chapter is like a dish; it has its own flavor and sauce. It has its song, its mood, its joy, and its despair.

It's the soundtrack of my life, and I'm damn proud of it. It sounds, tastes, and smells like effort, cold cigarettes, warm beer, and a profound detestation of defeat. But it also sweats pain, regrets, mistakes, wandering, and redemption. All this is seasoned with a huge dose of self-mockery and a few hits with a shovel when needed
Yeah, it burns, it swears, and it curses, but it's alive.

This book is the story of a man searching for his dignity. The kind you lose in drugs and booze and stitch back up with the tip of a chef's knife.
A no-filter, raw, unapologetic take on stupidity, people, and this insane world.
And above all: on this completely unhinged job.
It's a manifesto against boredom, exhaustion, and resignation.
Against an existence without passion—which is nothing but a slow death. A quiet agony.
I found salvation in packed dining rooms and in the flames of a kitchen. If it was possible for a lost cause like me, then it's possible for others too.
Because happiness... is a choice.
And tonight, it's on the menu.

Now that we've had a couple of cocktails, I will serve you the first course of the tasting menu.
Let's get to it.
I am sending the appetizer with the announcement of my own implosion, which started with ♫ *Let's Go Crazy* by Prince.

When everything collapsed in my life and I had nothing left to lose, he became my funky preacher.
His sermon?
In a world that's shutting down, celebrate life with passion and go nuts. Forget the rules and make noise. Raise hell and scream that you don't give a damn anymore.
And since my heart was in pieces and my brain already tainted.
I took him literally.
I snapped.
And lost my mind.

The origins of Evil

Some flames never die; They burn you slowly from childhood. A quiet fire that scorches everything over time.
In my case, the combustion smelled like Italian cuisine and a sense of abandonment and loneliness.
A particular song truly paints that feeling. One I still listen to repeatedly to this very day:
♫ *In a Nutshell* by Alice in Chains. Especially the unplugged version.
But now, at fifty-four, I hear it differently.
I finally get the subtext, and it sticks to me like the stench of my apron after a double shift.
Those lyrics reek of bad choices, regret... and that stubborn, ridiculous urge to keep existing anyway.
If you want to talk about a downward spiral—there it is.
Layne Staley's voice, spectral and hypnotic, pours like heroin oozing from a needle: warm, powerful, and lethal.
The track is dark and sad, and it suffocates you.
It's echoing either my birth or my own downfall.
I'm not even sure anymore.
Maybe both.
Only a guy who's hit rock bottom and clawed his way back can shake you like that.
I know what I'm talking about.
I know how it feels.
That's why it hits me that hard.

Let's start with a proper introduction.
My name is Alexandre Fenot.
I am French.
You can call me Alex. Actually you should.
Because I know it's a bitch to pronounce it in English. Trust me, after twenty years in the USA, I got used to being Alex. It was this or having it butchered in every sentence.
I was born April nineteenth, nineteen seventy-two, in Versailles, Yvelines. A fancy suburb about twenty minutes from Paris.
I received my official eviction notice from the womb on a Wednesday morning at eight o'clock sharp.
I come from a family of business owners.

My father.
He owned nightclubs and restaurants.
He was charming and seductive. But reckless, unhinged, and irresponsible.
The kind of guy who'd chase after someone who'd just stabbed him, sprinting four blocks with the knife still sticking out of his gut. True story.
He did his share of damage with my mother.
So she left with me under her arm when I was eight. Then they got divorced.
Officially for a complete lack of interest of the child.
It's cute to pin this on him, because both shared the same total absence of parental instinct and the same indifference toward their own kid.

Proof is he never once tried to reach out to me after she bailed.
I only saw him again thirty-eight years later.
He hadn't changed much, still kind, still smiling.
Still carrying that easygoing charm despite age and cancer.
But unfortunately still clueless and estranged from the concept of fatherhood.
His absence ripped me apart.
Go explain to an eight-year-old kid why his father is not in the picture.
Some parents do. In my case nobody did.
So people around me shut up and let the silence rot. And I grew up convinced it was my fault. That if I hadn't been born, my parents would've stayed together.
It's bullshit, of course.
But when nobody tells you the truth, you start believing the lies you make up to survive.
And once that poison is in you, good luck ever feeling whole again. Trust me, it's hard to be careless when you think your very existence ruined everything around you.
I dragged that dead weight for forty years until I finally understood that the problem wasn't about me. Well, at least not this time.
It was about them.
Anyway, since he wasn't around for most of my life, I am not going to spend two pages on him.
Let's move on.

As for my mother...
Where do I start?

What can I say?
She was beautiful, elegant, and educated.
But she was about as comfortable being a mom as a toddler with a blowtorch.
She had a smile that could melt the ice cap.
Except when it came to me.
Every time she looked at me, that smile vanished, and she was a bit colder and more distant.
Guess my face reminded her of her ex-husband.
I will pay for that insult my whole life.
Her fucking Yorkshire terriers, though, got all the attention.
That's precisely the time I built up my lifelong hatred of those little noisy rats. I can't stand lapdogs. Every time I hear one yapping with that high-pitched voice, I freak out.
It took me years to make peace with dogs, but I did later. You'll see. Be patient.
Actually, they're the only ones I ever reconciled with.

I inherited my father's craziness and inconsistency and my mother's temperament.
And since I screwed up plenty and carried a heavy past, our relationship eventually slowly turned toxic. Until it broke completely.
We stopped talking.
No discussion. No agreement.
Just... silence.
Call it a non-aggression pact or a kind of unspoken ceasefire.
No contact, no conflict.
You can't hurt what you don't see, right?

It's been over fifteen years now that I'm basically an orphan by choice and by principle.
And I don't blame her. I don't hate her; I just don't care anymore. She had her reasons. And with time, I've got mine as well to justify the silence. And this one?
It's not going anywhere.
It'll stay like that until one of us is gone. Or until it's too late.
Because we're the same: stubborn and ruthless. Let's say forgiveness and indulgence aren't in our DNA. Neither of us is worth redeeming on this. So we're both fine with it, and we live with it. especially her. She made that very clear.
I know, because somebody shoved it in my face. She's never even met my wife or my kids, but thanks to Facebook and Instagram, she knows exactly who they are.
I thought it was over, so I made peace with it. But something happened recently that brought the sparks back on and lit a raging fire inside me. And it's something I don't recommend, because I can hold a grudge like nobody's business.
Here's an anecdote that'll tell you everything you need to know about my dear mother.

Two years ago, my wife and daughter were on vacation in Sint Maarten, in the Caribbean.
They are having lunch at a beach restaurant.
And by pure coincidence—guess who's sitting two tables away?
My mother.
They had never met. So no history. No tension.

But do you think she said hello? A smile? A nod? Nope.
She kept her sunglasses welded to her face, sipping rosé, chain-smoking, and pretending not to see them.
Later, as she was swimming back to her fancy boat, my daughter, Rafaelle, actually swam next to her, trying to shake things up a bit to get her attention.
What do you think happened?
Nothing. Zero. Squat.
Not a word, not even a look.
And she had no reason to do that; they hadn't done anything to her.
Imagine if they had.
Rafaelle cried for two hours straight. It broke her heart.
Not sure what you think about that, but to humiliate your thirteen-year-old granddaughter like that, as far as I am concerned, you've got to be operating at a professional level of cruelty.
Or...
You have to be a world-class cunt.

Later that day, my wife, Peggy—I'll introduce her properly later—calls me and says to me:
— Ok. Now I get it. Now I see why you're always on edge, raw. Tough outside, mush inside. Indeed, it all makes sense now.

Moral of the story:
Rafaelle wanted to meet her. Done.
She wanted to talk to her... that didn't happen.

As for me, that little episode sealed it. I swore I'd never see my mother again while I'm alive or while she is, either.
So if my daughter still wants to meet her someday, it'll be after I'm gone.
Assuming she's still around.
And since I'm such a kind soul—that's me being sarcastic—I made my wife promise that if I croak before the witch, she's persona non grata at my funeral.
Not on the guest list. That's it.

There you go, Marie-Louise. That's all you deserve.
Oh, right, fun detail. I forgot that juicy part.
That's her real name. She always hated it, so she rebranded herself "Sandra" years ago.
Not to me.
After what she did to my daughter, she'll always be Marie-Louise.
One last thing, because this is where it gets tricky:
If I ever run into her, I'll do exactly what she did.
Walk past her without a glance or a word. Even if we're eating at facing tables, I'll ignore her with cold, merciless indifference and surgical precision.
What does that say about me?
That I inherited her gift for cruelty.
That we're both pros at being heartless and insensitive.
Like mother, like son.
The apple doesn't fall far away from the tree.

Anyway.
Where the fuck was I?
Crap, I lost the thread.
You see? Just mentioning Marie-Louise, and I'm already off balance.
It probably calls for a therapy session.
Maybe in another life.
Right, childhood.
My childhood memories are blurry and a bit hazy. The only things that stand out crystal clear are my grandmother and my uncle.

Jean-François. Jef.

I adored him.
He meant everything to me: a friend, a role model, a father figure. He was handsome, funny, strong, kind... and a little nostalgic and sensitive. Another decadent soul of the restaurant industry. He never really cared for my mother's emotional emptiness.
One day they fought and they stopped talking to each other. I am not even sure what they argued about. Not even sure they knew themselves.
But it's around that time that he found out he was sterile. It broke him. For a guy who loved kids and always wanted one—that hit hard.
One day, out of the fucking blue, he left Paris and moved to Sint Maarten. Yeah...that same island.
I think he wanted a fresh start. Maybe some air, some distance. Maybe to get away from certain people or something.
I'll never know.

Because I never saw him again.
He died at thirty-six years old in a motorcycle accident. He was hit by a car driven by a woman without a license.
I was eighteen.
I never really got over it.
It broke my heart.
Even writing this brings me tears.
Jef, you have no idea how much I miss you.

Alright.
Now let's meet the empress of stew
Rosa Maria Ambanelli, my grandmother.
The goddess of the stove, the mafia don of the stockpot.
She was a kind, caring person.
And everything started in her kitchen.

Oh yeah, side note:
Take a splash of Italian, a dash of Polish, and a hint of Normandie, and you have me.
A mutt seasoned with salted butter.
Stubborn, proud, hard-headed, and vindictive.
That'll come in handy later.

For reasons nobody ever explained to me, my mother dropped me there after the divorce. Like a duffel bag dumped at the luggage storage.
So, I lived for a while at Étain, a little town near Verdun.
Yep, it screams war and conflict. Guess I was programmed for battle, built for chaos.

That's also where my first of many addictions started.
As soon as the second school ended, I ran home with a backpack heavier than my whole life. Legs shot, underwear wetter than a November in Seattle. I opened the door, and then I'd burst through the door and head straight to the kitchen for my fix.
A full-blown olfactory explosion.
Not just smells but a molecular symphony.
The real stuff.
It smelled like heaven.
I'd stand by the stove, drooling. tongue practically out. I was tall enough to see the pots but too short to see what was inside, so my nose became my compass.
The house stank of honest and noble food.
Fresh gnocchi.
Creamy polenta with mascarpone
Intergalactic lasagna.
Osso buco from another dimension.
Warm rhubarb tart.
And that smell of fresh-ground coffee meant tiramisu was on the way.

That's when I realized eating isn't just stuffing your belly. It's a ritual. It's a mass.
It's a religion.
And I was in full conversion mode. I was a believer.
So I set up camp in that sacred place to do my homework—though not the kind they expected.

But I watched her, absorbed everything, and wanted to learn every trick of that black magic.
The kitchen became my fortress.
My church.
And she, my high priestess.
Amen.

Some time later, my mother came back for me.
Why?
How?
Why was I left there in the first place?
Why did she suddenly want me back?
No idea. To this day, no one ever gave me any explanation. That's still a fucking mystery.
So, I am back to living with my dear ghost-mother, plus a bonus prize: a stepdad.
Actually, let me correct that.
It feels strange calling him my stepfather.
He raised me like his own.
And I still see him as a father.
There. That's settled.

Claude

A good man. He raised me the best he could.
Sharp. Smart. Smooth talker, the kind that could sell sand to Saudis.
He was in retail—clothing. the expensive and fashionable kind.
He started from scratch, worked his ass off, and became successful in his field. We lived well, very comfortably. Wealthy.

Credit where it's due: I never lacked for anything material. They never denied me anything.
Except the essentials: attention and affection.
Warmth.
Plenty of money but not much psychology.
Again, to be fair and honest, I wasn't exactly a walk in the park.

There were two things I admired about Claude:
His kindness.
And his style...
The Dude dressed like royalty. Refined, elegant, and flawless taste.
When he left for work, I loved sneaking into his dressing room. I'd sit on the floor and just stare at the perfectly tailored suits, the ridiculously expensive shoes, and that collection of luxury watches.
One day, I even took one to school—just to show off.
He must have noticed, because later that morning, he showed up at my school. He walks in the class and asks me to step out into the hallway.
He looks at me and goes,
— What time is it?
At first, I'm thinking... that's a long trip just to ask me the time. Maybe you're not that smart after all.
Wait, it gets worse.
And what do I do?
I look at the watch... and tell him the time.
Like an absolute idiot.
Small detail: I had his Cartier Santos on my wrist.
That's the exact second it hit me:

I'd just screwed myself.
Checkmate.
A brilliant move on his part.

That's when my obsession with food really started to take shape.
Here's what a typical week looked like at my house back then:
Most of the time we had catered meals from Lenôtre or Flo Prestige. Two famous gourmet food shops at the time in Paris.
Fridays and Saturdays, we had dinner at restaurants.
And Sunday: pasta... overcooked.
No, let's be fair: hammered.
No one cooked at home for two reasons.
First, my mother was a pathological clean freak. Borderline clinical. She hated stains, spills, and smells. Anything that made a kitchen feel alive.
Second—and let's thank her for that—she sucked at cooking. Her food was as awful as my grandmother's was divine.
So, with time, I have developed a permanent trauma toward takeout and catering. And I still do to this day.
But restaurants... It was a different story.
The second I stepped into one, I was hypnotized.
An early, almost unnatural attraction.
Not without consequences for later.
Sunday nights, When I was lying in bed, I had one obsession:
Where are we going for dinner next Friday?

When my parents worked late, I was alone, so I became independent quickly and learned to cook for myself. I rotated between elbow pasta with ham and cheese, instant mashed potatoes with ground beef, and my two personal chefs:
Mr. William Saurin" for canned sausages with lentils and for one of my favorite dishes ever: cassoulet.
And Mr. "Buitoni" for meat-stuffed ravioli in tomato sauce.

I tamed solitude and even found some comfort in it. But after a while, it weighed on me.
I started feeling neglected. Forgotten.
So I did what I knew best: I went headfirst into rebellion, as some enter the convent.
I was a world-class slacker and got expelled from several schools. But not because I was dumb, because I was a mouthy pain in the ass—cocky, arrogant, and already carrying the ego of a Banana Republic general.
My priorities?
Food. My buddies. My Walkman. My bike.
Not exactly Harvard material.
I collected troubles like it was a hobby, and my parents fumed; they were pissed, disappointed, and bitter.
And one day they threw it at me:
— You'll end up in a dead-end job... server or in a kitchen.
Prophecy? Clairvoyance?
I've been in the restaurant business for thirty years and on both sides of the pass.

So mission accomplished.
Impressive, right?

I kept going to school, but I had zero interest in higher education. I was stuck.
But destiny, that funny fucker, gave me a shove—if you can call it that.
Barely twenty, I was scouted on the street, and someone offered me a shot at modeling.
I sold the idea to my parents. They agreed, happy to stop wasting money on private schools I kept getting kicked out of.
Timing was perfect; I was full of myself: good-looking, tall, and skinny like a promise in a Weight Watchers commercial. I was offered all seven sins on a silver platter and the chance to be the center of attention. Famous. Superficial. Seen.
I got my revenge.
Finally.

What do they say about having dinner with the devil?
You can go, but you need to use a very long spoon.
Fuck it, I sat at the table and grabbed the food with my bare hands, and I dove in headfirst.
Runways, photo shoots, magazine covers, and TV shows. I even had a fan club. My face was plastered on magazines and billboards in the streets.
I had the dream team, the fantasy anyone would kill for: fame, money, coke, women, and exclusive nightclubs.
But it did not fill the hole inside.

The city wasn't big enough to fill the emotional void.
Paris. London. Milan. Madrid. For four years, I dragged my vanity around like a Vuitton suitcase.
I lived in another dimension, in the Twilight Zone. And I lost touch with reality.
I was living in a bubble.
But it was about to blow up in my face.
And when it did, the ground slid out from under me.
And... I fell into a black hole.

After four years of full-scale self-destruction, I knew I had to stop.
So, I decided I had to take a hard turn and quit while I still can.
I walked away from my shining career, despite the promises of an easier life and more spotlight.
I looked for an escape plan.
An exit
And trust me—in my case, it was a fucking emergency.

P.S.
During those wasted years, I lost touch with my grandmother.
She passed away before I could say goodbye.
Yeah, I fucked that up too.
That's one of the things I'll never forgive myself for.
It still haunts me.

Service not included

In the early nineties, I landed in New York for the first time in my life to see my best friend, David, who just moved there.
The Big Apple... the most electrifying city in the world.

At that time, ♫ *Bad* by U2 was on repeat in my headphones while I was wandering through this concrete jungle.
A decadent, pathetic, yet beautiful track.
A dizzying trip about addiction that digs into my soul every time I hear it.
A sharp, haunting guitar riff.
A fragile voice screaming without ever breaking.
On the edge, hanging on by a thread.
Like me.

I spend hours walking. I am a movie freak, so I feel like I am on a film set at every damn corner.
The thing is, I am fresh off the plane, perfumed by the smell of French baguette and bad intentions.
And Manhattan is about to blow my whole life in pieces.
But more importantly, this is the beginning of my journey into this insane industry. That trip is a front-row seat at the greatest circus on earth: New York's dining scene.
Restaurant concepts built like acid trips where people aren't just cooking; they are plating dishes with feverish frenzy, possessed by an incredible creative energy. Pure madness.

Then one day, as I was strolling down Broadway, I drifted into the Virgin Megastore at Times Square (yeah, Gen Z, it used to be a thing).
And I come across a book.
On the cover, a chef.
One of those "gods in white jackets."
But this one... He didn't look friendly or polished.
He had a hard stare
The kind of look Keith Richards would give you if you handed him a ukulele and asked him to play an Aerosmith hit.
You get the picture?
The title:
Anthony Bourdain – Kitchen Confidential.
And holy shit, what a shock.
He wasn't talking about gastronomy or fine dining. but about junkies of mise en place, high on rush.
Gladiators of the service.
Fragile, broken, and doomed cooks, breathing in the flames of the kitchen.
Every word was a punch in the gut, every page was a brick thrown at the intellectual masturbation that was starting to suck the soul out of kitchens.
He didn't give a damn about rules, respectability, or polished culinary storytelling. He was an outlaw, a misfit. A pirate who made it possible to walk through hell without getting scorched.
He was chaos with a conscience.
He turned the kitchen brigade into a goddamn punk band.

Forget the lukewarm jazz-rock trio of fancy dinners.
This was food, drugs, and fuck-you sauce.
A greasy truth, spiced with heroin, served on a chipped plate.
It was a revelation; it was like being told that you can be lost, wrecked, or beat up, but if you work right, you belong. And even if you are broken or messed up, you can still shine.
Lost, messed up, damaged.
That's me, goddammit! Where do I sign?
I devoured that book like you'd eat a juicy rib eye after six months of veganism.
And just like that, I went back to Paris with that bible still echoing in my head like a nasty slap on the ear.
I knew what I had to do and what I wanted to do.
My father was a restaurant owner, and my two uncles were chefs, so...
Karma? Instinct? Destiny?
Pick your poison.

On top of that, from time to time, I'd run into another monster of charisma. A person who will become, without even knowing it, a model.
A reference point.
Back then, during some rare moments of sobriety and clarity, I had the honor of meeting giants.
David's wife, Caroline, was the daughter of a man who, without me even realizing it, became a reference point.
Monsieur Michel Rostang.

What a man!
A lord of French cuisine.
A gentleman chef.
In his white jacket, he commanded respect. No one made a sound in his kitchen. Even when we came by before service to say hello, it was bows, reverence, and total devotion.
Outside his kitchen, his voice was calm and steady. He was elegant and generous. Kind.
I got dragged a few times into insane meals where you had thirty Michelin-starred chefs sitting around a whole roasted pig, reminiscing about the good old days.
And let me tell you, on the menu, you could look all you wanted... there was no quinoa on the horizon.
And if you wanted water? There was a garden hose out back.
The cherry on top?
Rostang, Dutournier, and all their peers, shirtless, in shorts and suspenders, a glass of cognac in hand, laughing their asses off while playing pétanque.
That had style.
An authenticity we don't see anymore.
That wild bunch made me realize this is my world.
So I choose the restaurant industry as a lifeline.
I didn't become a cook right away.
Not yet.
But I had the smell, the scar, and the damn calling.
The needle was already in the vein.
So I jump in.

I applied at La Butte Chaillot.
The owner is Guy Savoy. A great chef—simple, respectful.
The place is an upscale bistro, Avenue Kléber. Right in the middle of high society territory in Paris.
Funny detail: it's also my parents' hangout.
So the day I show up to give my so-called resume, the staff already know who I am.
The manager asks me:
— You come from a rich family, you're a model, you're sure you really want to be a waiter?
I tell him:
—It's this or nothing. And I'm not leaving without the job.
They hire me.
Out of kindness? Not only.
As the waiters there are a bit gruff, it doesn't hurt having a good-looking kid, well-groomed, who knows how to talk to the fancy clientele.

I know the menu by heart already; we eat there at least once a week. But I spend my first day just watching.
I study the waiters. Their habits. Their flow.
I figure out how the system works; I learn the ropes and the sections.
I may be a professional slacker with an attitude, but I am sly. So my reptilian brain switched on.
I analyze everything.
How do I cut corners and go faster?

How to take on the habit of never leaving the dining room empty-handed.
How they take orders.
Fire the tables.
Clear a table of six without taking two trips.
How to stack plates, silverware, etc.
Anything to save time.
And most importantly, how to talk to the chef.

After two shifts of observing, the next day I tell them I am ready. So they give me the smallest station with an old-timer to watch over me.
I work like a man on a mission and almost doubled the tips thanks to my ultra-bright, overly polite smile. Which works like magic with my slick manners.
Within a month, I'm part of the furniture.
I am adopted by the cooks because I am a nut job, and the servers are happy as we split the tips.
But my success didn't stop there.
Female customers love that charming idiot who serves them their plates with a look that screams trouble.
I am a magnet for Daddy's little rich girls and bored divorcées looking to play with fire.
I collect phone numbers scribbled on the back of receipts. And once the service is done, we meet for a drink sometimes at a bar, sometimes at the fancy hotel across the street.
A palace that will become like my second home.
Now, don't get the wrong idea.
I never took a dime, never accepted a thing in return. I wasn't a gigolo.

The truth is, I was too dumb and too proud for that.
Maybe that's what made me look so attractive and "dangerous." Because I didn't want anything in return.
In fact, it's the first thing my wife told me when we met:
—You, you're dangerous.
For me, it was about the beauty of the game.
Yeah, I had a sense of duty.
If somebody has to sacrifice in the name of lust,
♫ *let it be me* (a little nod to Ray LaMontagne).
And one day the manager asked me,
— So, how are your parents doing?
Yeah... they stopped showing up now that I work there. They switched restaurants.
Imagine the embarrassment; you're part of the Parisian elite, and your son's the one serving you.

Over time, my file got thicker because I traded shifts like a fucking maniac. I filled in for all the guys who didn't want to tire themselves.
And on top of that, I kept up my bullshit on the side, carrying bad habits from my days in the spotlight.
The second service is done; I run off to fry my brain in clubs where regular people couldn't even look at the door.
Why? For nothing.
Just for fun.
Just for the sheer satisfaction of destroying myself on both fronts.

After three years like that, I start going a little schizophrenic.
And even if my pay isn't great, I live like a spoiled brat. I keep dodging the tabs thanks to my angel face, my sadistic gaze, and my egotistic attitude.
But deep down, I know:
I'm not looking for a job.
I'm looking for a refuge.
A family.
And I find it in the three p.m. cigarette on the sidewalk.
In the filthy jokes between waiters and in the chaos of a slammed service.
And most of all, in that shared mindset that we are together. That we are not there to be adored but to push through, to deliver, no matter what.

Then I am transferred to the "Cap Vernet."
Another spot of Guy Savoy, Rue Vernet, in the eighth district.
A huge restaurant with two floors.
So, I keep rolling with it; I like the place, but something's missing. I feel boredom creeping in.
Six months in, one night, I've got a section on the mezzanine.
I am a little more wasted than usual, and as I go down the stairs, I miss the first step. And I tumble down the entire staircase with a tray full of oysters.
I land on my ass covered with oysters, ice, and seaweed. And a twisted ankle.
Of course, everyone is laughing their asses off.
Not me.

I limp home, smelling like low tide and furious.
Because my ego couldn't handle the humiliation.
I spend a few days stewing in my apartment.
The day I can walk again, I go back to the restaurant and quit.
I can already hear the shitty jokes every time I'd go up or down those fucking stairs.
I was planning to leave the restaurant anyway.
Not in such a ridiculous way, of course. Maybe with a little more dignity. Whatever.
So I am hunting for something flashier, more glamorous. Somewhere with glitter and chaos.
But I swear that though I botched my exit at the last place, I would nail my entrance at the next one.
Literally and figuratively.
And I did.

I land at the Hôtel Costes as a head waiter. At the time, it was the trendiest and hottest restaurant in Paris. The kind where they charge you the ice cubes and the air you breathe. I am a perfect fit.
My first day... unforgettable.
I show up in full swagger through the front door, the main entrance, the one for guests.
No one says anything because thanks to my stepfather, I've got a killer wardrobe: Hugo Boss, Armani, and all of it. So they think I'm a client.
Once I am clocked in, the manager comes over.
Cool guy, just doing his job.
But since someone saw me come in through the "wrong" door, he has to give me the talk:
— Hey, big guy.

I'm six-three, and the boss can't stand tall people, so "Big Guy" stuck as my nickname.
He continues:
– You can't come in that way; you have to use the back service entrance, the staff door.
I smile, and I am about to answer him when he feels the need to add this:
– Like everybody else.
Ouch, big mistake;
That was the only thing not to say.
I give him a killer glare, wipe the smile off my face, and shoot back:
– Oh yeah? Well, I'm not everyone else.
And I go back to work.
The servers who heard me are stunned, and the guy is just standing there, floored by such nerve.
I do my shift, and he observes me like some kind of weird animal.
At the end of the night, before I leave, he repeats the rules. Rules that, by the way, don't apply to managers. That triggers something in me.
I am on mutiny mode.

The next day, just to be sure to make my point, I go ballistic and come in through that very same door. But with a worse attitude.
I make my entrance in a three-piece suit and a beige cashmere coat, with a slow, swinging, confident walk and a predatory smile.
You remember Travolta strutting down the street to ♫ *Stayin' Alive* in Saturday Night Fever?
Well, that was me. At the peak of my arrogance and stupidity.

Heads turn.
Hostesses melt.
Clients stare.
Waiters are cracking up.
The manager? Not so much.
He snaps:
— I thought I told you...
I cut him off cold.
— Yeah. You did ask me nicely. But no, I prefer that entrance. Is that going to be a problem?
He looks at me and understands instantly. There is nothing he can do. I am a lost cause. So he sighs and mutters,
— Forget it; it's fine.
Defeated.

From there, I stand out fast.
I quickly make a name for myself. And despite all the VIPs in the restaurant, the only star in the room is me. My inflated ego spares no one.
The staff treats me like royalty. Probably because I always have dope on me, and the bartender keeps sending me cocktails, which I pass around like communion wine.
There, among the happy few, the coke, the booze, and a packed restaurant, the schedule and the energy are pure chaos.
With all the noise I make, the customers think I am management. So the servers come up with a plan:
When someone screws up, instead of getting yelled at by the manager, they come to me.

I go to the table, do my routine, and smooth it over. And if there is a problem with the kitchen, I go talk to the chef. He likes me, so it always works out.
And when the manager asks what was going on, we all say in unison
— Just helping a colleague.
And he nods.
It works
I'm impossible to manage, but I'm a damn good waiter. A machine. Fast. Efficient. Strong seller. And I thrive in pressure, conflicts, and daily mayhem.

But behind that apparent success on the floor, I am hiding a total wreck inside. Emotionally, I'm a mess, and I am split right down the middle.
A rock star waiter at night, doing my full-house performances. And an empty shell by day, brain-fried by all my excesses.
I need a jolt, something to snap me out of this gnawing feeling that is eating me alive.
I'm rotting from the inside.
So, after a year there, I ask to be promoted to manager since I am basically already doing the job.
And that's when it hit: the ice-cold shower.
They flat-out refused.
The fuckers denied me the promotion.
But at least they happily provide me an explanation. To rub my nose in it.

I am too cocky. Too loud. I take up too much space. and most importantly, I've pissed off too many people. I've stepped on too many toes.
So much for thinking I was appreciated and liked.
It turns out my popularity is... relative.
I learned the hard way that respect isn't given or bribed.
You earn it.
I'll never, ever forget that lesson.

So after service, I hand in my two weeks' notice.
Fuck it. I will take my talent and my bullshit somewhere else.
What about across the street?
Right in front of them.

Brass and bullshit

The Fool's Marching Band

I guess the title of this chapter might sound a little weird to you.
Well, it's actually pretty simple.
Back then, I was a full-blown marching band all by myself.
Every entrance was a racket of lies, a carnival of bullshit louder than the truth itself.
I had the flute slung over my shoulder, blowing horseshit like a virtuoso.
I strutted with my recorder because I had the swagger for it.
And between my legs I carried a big drum, a reminder I had the balls not to back down.
So there was no need for an orchestra; I already had the whole damn kit and the costumes for a grotesque parade.
The result? A harmonious mess.
Did it sound off? Sometimes.
But I was the conductor of my own crooked symphony.
And since we're talking about percussion, let's cue the music.
Back then I had my own anthem.
In our playlist go to the letter G.
G as Gainsbourg.

And let's play the ♫ *Requiem pour un con.*

Yeah, I know, it's French.
So I am going to make a quick note for the non-French speakers:

The word "con" is a bitch to translate. It's not exactly a fool, not exactly an asshole. It's worse. Both pathetic and abrasive at the same time. Stupid, arrogant, and ridiculous, all rolled into one. Even if you spit it like venom, then "fool" gets you only halfway there.
Listen, you've got songs about losers (Beck), assholes (Denis Leary), bad boys (George Thorogood), and even toxic exes (Carly Simon). But trust me, this song hits harder than anything you guys ever wrote in English. No one crucified fools like Gainsbourg did.
Two minutes of raw truth.
A simple beat, just a drum kit, a guitar riff, a bass line, and words hurled like a cigarette butt in your face.
So yeah. Requiem for a fool,
Fitting choice, right?
Especially for a guy like me.
Let's move on.

The day after I quit Costes, someone tells me the Park Hyatt Vendôme is looking for a restaurant general manager. It has just opened, and it's the new jewel of the Pritzker family, Hyatt's owners. Turns out, it's the new hotspot in Paris. One hundred meters from my old job.
Great news, but there is only one problem: I have zero experience in management.
No worries; if you think this will stop me, you're dead wrong.

I cook up a fake resume with the help of buddies working in other restaurants. And we agree on the story:
— Ok, if they call, you tell them I worked here and I was running the place.

I stop by and leave my resume.
Luckily for me, it's the F&B director who takes it. He tells me to come back later in the afternoon for an interview.
When I come back that day, I sit down with him, and I shoot for the stars. I go all in.
For two hours straight, I talk. Sell. I perform one of my best shows.
Then he tells me that he wants me to meet the hotel director. He introduces me to him, and we talk. I hypnotize him too.
They are both hooked.
And just like that... they offer me the job.
I'm about two seconds away from shitting myself, but I keep the act going.
I push the bluff even further, asking with a killer smile and a voice full of confidence,
—Do you need references?
Even though I am in pure panic inside.
They smile back to me and set me free by saying
—No, we can tell you're a professional.
Yeah, sure...
A professional bullshitter.

The pressure is maximum because I am running the main restaurant in the hotel.
And somehow... I made it work.

Because I find out that I have it in my blood. It's like second nature. I'm programmed and built for it. And when I don't know something, I stall and improvise. I read, I gather info, and I adapt. I work like a maniac to compensate for what I ignore.

I'm there from breakfast through continuous lunch service, straight into dinner, and in for the cocktail lounge late at night.

I handle everything and barely sleep four hours a night. I finish work at two in the morning, and I'm back on site at five for breakfast, checking the buffet setup and the deliveries.

Some days the hotel director, to thank me for the hard work, even gives me a room, and I crash for an hour or two. When I wake up, the hotel laundry has already cleaned and pressed my clothes.

Seven days a week, I am the first one to arrive and the last one to leave.

That's when something shifted.

Little by little I start developing a holy hatred for mediocrity and approximations.

So I become demanding. And I hold people to the same standard I hold myself to.

My enthusiasm becomes contagious, and I start pulling the team together. The staff begins to follow me and trust me. And even harder to understand... they actually start believing in me. The endless days and my shitty temper don't scare them off. The more I demand from them, the harder I push myself, and the more loyal they become.

I learned my lesson at Costes.

Speaking of which, since being modest has never really been my style, I can't help myself showing off. I am in the big league now, and my name starts to pop up on the restaurant's who's who in Paris.
So twice a week, right after the lunch service, I go there to eat and parade around.
The managers who pushed me out now have to serve me.
They fume.
I gloat.
"Asshole," you say?
Fuck yeah.

During this period, my life is a complete mess. But the moment I walk into the restaurant, I become calm and razor-sharp. I see everything. I control everything.
I don't even seem to have many physical limits. I work until exhaustion—which never comes. I absorb service after service like a machine. But eventually it's a waiter who cracks first.

One night, we're hosting the launch party for a book by the French-Greek TV anchor Nikos Aliagas, a big event. Packed room.
One of my servers is completely exhausted, nerves shot. burned out.
I ask him if he still wants to work the event.
He tells me he doesn't want to let me down. I

Assure him I wouldn't hold it against him if he leaves. But he doesn't want to disappoint me, so he stays.
My bad, wrong call. I should have been more careful. I missed the warning signs.
Rookie mistake.
I lose sight of him for about ten minutes.
Then he suddenly reappears, running through the dining room shirtless, wearing a bucket hat, and setting off a fire extinguisher in the middle of the happy few.
What follows is a full-blown wild chase through the restaurant. The security is trying to corner him, VIPs are shocked everywhere, and I'm running like a lunatic, laughing my ass off while trying at least to grab the extinguisher.
Once we finally catch him, the kid is, of course, fired on the spot.

You want burnout? There, you have it.
I'll come back to this later, because it matters—and very few people realize what this job really costs us.

The next day I called him and asked him to come by. I hand him a glowing recommendation letter—some "Employee of the Month" level bullshit.
He screwed up, sure, but I respected his devotion, his loyalty.
I can be an ass, for sure, but not a bastard.
There's a difference. Subtle, but real.

Later that year, it was my turn to cause another clusterfuck.
Every Wednesday we have the weekly directors' meeting. And that week's agenda is whether or not to change the name of the hotel's fine-dining restaurant.
To say I don't give a rat's ass about it is a euphemism.
The meeting starts, and everyone gives their clean, polished, PowerPoint-approved presentations.
Naturally, since nobody is talking about me or my outlet, I'm bored out of my mind.
And it shows.
The GM notices, looks at me, and says,
—Are we boring you?"
And I reply brutally:
— Yes.
Dead silence; you could hear a fly fart.
The director is stunned.
Then I go in:
— You're wasting your time over the name of a restaurant that does fifteen covers a day, costs a fortune, and brings in nothing. Meanwhile, I (yes, I put myself first on purpose) and my team are running a restaurant packed from six a.m. to two a.m. with a shitty name that sounds like a funeral hall. "Les Salons." I am sorry, but it sucks.
So if something needs to be changed, it's that.

Earlier that morning, I spoke to my F&B director about the idea. He agreed that it was a good idea,

but he begged me to drop it. He told me it was too risky and it was not the right time to go for it.
That I had to be patient.
Risky? Wrong timing?
Sounds like a job for me.
And patient?
That's cute; I like the word, but it's not my style.

After my "risky" outburst, I look at him.
He has his head in his hands, looking like he just watched his and my career go up in flames.
I know he likes me, but I know I crossed the line, and I am not sure if he's going to spend any overtime trying to save my ass.
The hell with it. Lost for lost, I double down and hold the fort for thirty-five minutes straight.
Ranting like a preacher on meth. When I am done, I wrap it up:
— If you want to keep jerking off over a restaurant that nobody gives a shit about, be my guest. I've got real work to do.
And I storm out.

Thirty minutes later, I am summoned to the top floor.
As I am walking towards the boardroom, I am expecting to be crushed and fired. I open the door and ... I get a standing ovation. Applause from the whole fucking jury, and the hotel director congratulates me.
I look at my F&B director; he just shakes his head and says to me, laughing:

— You're fucking insane, but you have balls. Though it's the way you are going to plan your career. I am officially worried.
I didn't give a shit.
I won.
Once again, I have shocked and offended everyone. But I have what I want.
They change the name of a restaurant. Mine.
The executive chef of the fine-dining spot is livid. He can't believe some loudmouth punk just stole his thunder.
Buddy, you may have a star on your menu—or on your door. But in here, there's only one.
Me.
He will never speak to me again.

A few months later, things are going off the rails for good.
One day, David walks in mid-service in the restaurant, out of breath and in panic mode.
— Tomorrow, the Stones are playing across the street, at the Olympia. It was just announced thirty minutes ago; we have to line up for tickets NOW!
I run upstairs to tell the GM I have to leave.
He flat-out refuses. Telling me if I walk out, I am putting my career in jeopardy. Especially since I am next in line to take over as F&B director—the current one is being promoted overseas. He advises me to keep my head down and keep my nose clean. Otherwise, I am done.
Yeah, right, not a chance.

Come on, between my rent, my job, and the Rolling Stones...
What do you think I picked?
The Stones, of course.
So I quit on the spot.
I walk out of his office and head to the restaurant, where I found my buddy. As I tell him the problem is solved, he smiles.
Since he is just as dumb as I am, he has just quit two hours earlier after his boss had been busting his balls as well.
It"s a good thing our priorities are in sync.
So we leave, arms locked in, smiling like a pair of proud idiots.

I have another job in another trendy restaurant soon after. But my life is all about sharp suits and wild nights. And of course, the holy trinity: work, booze, and cocaine.
Not always in that order, but always together.
And the more I work, the more I use.

And yet, every single morning, the moment I walk into work, brain fried from the night before, soul running on fumes, I am doing the same thing over and over. I stop by the kitchen to say hi to the cooks. I am obsessed with them. Hypnotized.
No matter where I worked, no matter which restaurant, I have always been staring at them quietly for a while.
I am jealous of those gods in white.
They are down there in the pit of hell, while I am floating in the paradise of vice.

I watch them burn with purpose, with discipline, through a chaos that somehow makes sense. While I am burning too. But from within. And for nothing.

Back then, being a cook wasn't sexy.
No followers, no stupid emoji stars.
You were a hick. A grunt.
A billboard for school failure.
But me? I stared at them like they were rock stars.
It wasn't a brigade; it was a fucking tribe.
A clan.
They insulted each other, threw pans, and sometimes even fought. And five minutes later, they were laughing again.
They were bonded by napalm.
And at the head of that army of lunatics stood the chef. The only guy whose name was stitched on his jacket. When he barked a command, the whole brigade shouted back in unison:
– YES, CHEF!
Hearing that, I had chills straight to my underwear.
Everyone in the dining room kept their distance from him. But not me.
I couldn't take my eyes off the guy.
He had this insane charisma. He was calm, composed, and an indisputable authority.
When shit hit the fan, he didn't flinch. He just absorbed it and kept going.
One night I walked into the kitchen to sniff the beast and asked him,
—Is everything alright, Chef?

He looks at me with a manic smile and those laser eyes and said,
– No choice in the kitchen, kid. We have to make it work.
That mix of madness and resolve leaves me speechless. I admire the hell out of him. He is my hero.
I never forgot him.

And in all that chaos, one thought kept gnawing: Paris is too small for me.
Another fucking brilliant mistake.
I am offered a position at “Nobu" in London.
I lasted a month, just enough for the training and the hipsters' managers to piss me off.
So I walk out. But I stay in London and work in a different restaurant for a while.
I didn't keep great memories from that time and that city. Shitty weather, shitty food, shitty accent.
The truth is, I haven't really changed a thing in my life. I just moved my circus to a new city, but it's the same clown act.
And in London, there is vodka, coke, and girls.
So, I keep getting high and keep sinking down. deeper and deeper.
In a last attempt to tank my career for good, lose all common sense, and bury my moral compass once and for all. I decide to move to the ultimate paradise of vanity and addiction.
The island where my parents have their little empire and their names glowing in gold letters on restaurants' VIP books.
St. Barts.

Two days after landing, I run into my mother by accident in a supermarket.
We are already estranged at that point, but she still throws this dagger at me. She shoots at me, cold as ice:
— What the fuck are you doing on my island?
I look at her, smile, and walk away without a word.
It is one of the last times we will ever face each other. I think the very last was December thirtieth of that same year.
Anyway, I take over the restaurant in a hotel owned by a friendly guy.
Only one little problem: he is just as lost as me but in a different way.
He is the ex-husband of a local legend, and he wants to prove he exists without her.
Me?
I just want to reign.
Chaos is my kingdom, and I rule it proudly.
He has more money, but I am unbeatable in stupidity. My superiority complex is stratospheric.

The worst part?
I am good at reading restaurants—I can see instantly what works and what doesn't.
It's like a superpower.
Same with people. I smell them and decode them, and I am rarely wrong.
It works on everyone—except me.
I ignore my flaws. My darkness.

I refuse to see that my demons and my obsession with shining at all costs are steering me straight into a wall.
I have a vague recollection of sensing the end coming. I was starting to feel the overload.
The crash.
I was destroying myself so much and so fast that I'd stopped even being good at my job. I was done, cooked.
I didn't just hit rock bottom. I took a fucking lease. I lived there. I slept there.
And yet, nothing's ever fully written, even when you think it's over. Because I was about to take the biggest slap of my life.
One that would change everything.
Forever.

PS:

You'll understand that I hesitated with 🎵 *Hell Ain't a Bad Place to Be* by AC/DC for the soundtrack of this chapter.
Looking back, yeah, it was brutal. It was chaos, complete madness, but it was also one hell of a ride.
You deal with the wreckage later. Alone, staring in the mirror.
If you asked me now whether I'd do it all over again at the same age,
Change anything?
Ask a kid if he wants to get off the carousel or go for another round.
There's your answer.

The kamikaze in high heels

My grandmother used to say that there are two things I should never forget in life:
— If you put a donkey on a racetrack, the only thing it'll do is fuck up the grass.
The other one:
— If a man stands tall, it's because there's a woman behind, holding him up.
So, this chapter is the story of a woman who bet on a donkey, held him up, and dragged him onto a racetrack.
She knew I was a lost cause.
She could have chosen peace.
But she chose war by picking me.
And she jumped anyway, headfirst, into a free-fall kind of love.
Heart on fire, like a soldier on a suicide mission.
Stilettos as sharp as samurai blades.
My kamikaze in high heels.

Some days you wake up and feel it's going to be a shitty day. And when the day's over, as you were right, you think that you should have stayed in bed.
Well, for me it was the opposite.
Getting out of bed was the best decision I ever made. Because that day changed my whole life and flipped it upside down.

St. Barts, six p.m.

I am getting ready for dinner service. I have barely any reservations; it's going to be a slow night. I am already bored just thinking about it.
The phone rings:
– Alex, we're taking the boat and going to party in Sint Maarten. Are you in?
We're what? Am I in? You're kidding—ask a blind man if he wants to see.
Service is an hour away, so I grab my assistant and bullshit something about an emergency and I tell him,
– You're in charge, man. I have to split.
My friend has barely hung up the phone that I am already on the boat with half a gram of coke in my brain and four or five shots in my gut.
We take off at night, half-fried, like runaway teenagers. The crossing is going fine: calm sea, music blasting, vodka flowing.
We dock, grab a car, and head to a restaurant.
I climb up the few steps to the dining room, and then...

Her.
An apparition, half angel, half demon.
Take your pick.
A divine and diabolical creature, wearing a white silk dress that is clinging to her like temptation itself. Athletic, sexy, elegant, and with the aura of a war general.
She sees me and chooses me.
She looks me straight in the eyes, sharp enough to drill through my skull. Madness and tenderness in the same glance.

And my heartbeat explodes.
Fuck. It works. I'm not dead, not a zombie. Not completely, anyway.
It's love at first sight.
No question.
No hesitation.
Just... obvious.
I find out during dinner that the restaurant belongs to her parents. She's just giving a hand with the service.
Later that evening, she sits down right in front of me. I try to speak, but nothing comes out.
So, we talk in silence. We just look at each other.
We spend the evening like that, just staring.
I am choking; I can't eat, and I can't breathe.
The only thing I can do is drink as much booze as I can to find the courage to ask her out.
At the end of the meal, I do.
We leave together and do the rounds of clubs. We dance, drink, and party like animals. We don't let go of each other for a second.
Then we go back to the hotel and spend the night together, passionate, feverish, and intense.

The next morning, since there is no way I'm leaving her. I call the restaurant.
— I have food poisoning; I can't come to work.
We spend the week glued together like two grains of rice under the same lid.
And that's when I meet her kid.
He is four, with an angel's face and a maniac's stare. I know that look; it's familiar. I have the same.

We sized each other up and locked eyes. And I think at that moment we both have the same thought: This one is going to be a pain in my ass. Well, I finally understood what my parents felt when they looked at me.

She tells me she has to go back to Miami, where she lives. In a pure moment of delusion, I tell her that I want to follow her, be with her.
I have nothing to lose; I have no life and no future, so why the hell not?
Against all odds, she agrees.
So I do what I do best. I burn everything down to the ground. I go back to St. Barth, quit, and pack my bags.
Next thing you know, I'm in Miami.
—I'll take care of that city later. It deserves its own massacre. Don't worry, it's coming.—
We're living in her apartment, learning how to coexist, learning each other's rhythms. We circled each other, trying to fit.
She's a warrior, and I'm a wrecking ball, so sometimes it's tense; we crashed a couple of times, and sparks fly.
We get married. The papers played a role, but mostly because we are crazy about each other.
I'm too stupid to say I'm in love with her.
She's too in love to tell me to fuck off.
I am head over heels; she believes in me when neither I nor anybody else does.
She is everything I am not. She's calm, generous, and grounded.
I'm selfish. Defensive. Full of shit.

But with her, I can be better. I can change.
If I actually want to, that is.
But deep down I know that if I want to keep her by my side, I don't have the choice.
I don't exactly have much to bring to the table anyway. All I have to offer is a few chapters of a life defined by the glamour of the stamps on my passport. Paris, London, St. Barts, and Miami turned me into a jet-setting junkie. I'm hollow inside.

I get a restaurant manager gig in South Beach. I'm still boozing, still snorting, spiraling. Still falling deeper every damn day. as if it were humanly possible.
Then, a severe depression hits me and breaks me in half. I start avoiding mirrors. I can't stand what I see.
But I sweep everything under the rug.
I stack it. Bury it. Fake it. Whatever! Anything that allows me to pretend I am above water.
I'm not. And I've been drowning for a while.
But she doesn't quit. She holds on and she doesn't flinch.
This woman's got a mind of steel. She keeps moving, no matter what life throws at her. And with me, life throws hard.
I won't talk about her family or her past.
I don't own those rights; they're too expensive.
Let's say we were both dented. Both cracked.
Let's leave it there.

We have a daughter. Rafaelle.

I try to be a dad, but patience isn't my strongest suit. Because I don't have an ounce of it.
I'm working nights; I am barely home. But when I am, I'm either angry, cruel, bitter, distant... or just not interested.
The floods of love and its sweet perfume are not strong enough to kill the flames of hell. In other words, her friends and family are starting to flinch and brace in survival mode. With time, I think they are probably wondering what she sees in this narcissistic prick.
And at some point... I have to agree with them.
It's getting hard to find an excuse or defend a guy like me.

I hop jobs like I change underwear. Always burning out, moving on. And, one morning, I'm tapped out, at the end of my rope.
Desperate, yet lucid, for the first time in a while I want to fire my last shot... To salvage what can still be saved
Not out of pride or ego.
Not out of self-respect, because I don't have any left to spare.
But out of love, plain and simple.

***

No, your screen isn't frozen.
No, it's not an editing problem or a misprint.
That blank space? It's on purpose.
You'll get the reason in the next chapter.
***

I look at Peggy, a double espresso in hand, and I tell her I need a radical change. I am not happy anymore; my job bores me, and I want to be a chef.
— I'm done being miserable. This is my dream. It's time.
She smirks.
— Yeah? You don't have the balls to start over.
She knows exactly how to trigger me. She knows how to light the fuse.
And I can't resist a challenge. Never could.
This woman is sharp as hell. She figured me out. You don't fight a wild animal; you let it tire itself out. And me, I am rattled. I am going in circles in my cage, and I'm losing my mind out of spite and anger. I am tired of fighting everything and blaming the whole world instead of taking a look in the mirror.
She knew the only way out was through me.
And I finally got it.
That's how she saved my ass.
Again.

So I quit the cushy general manager position and started at the bottom. Rock-fucking-bottom.
I dump my illusions, my past, and my comfort in the trash. No title, no bullshit, no safety net.
I take a commis gig in a tiny, shabby French joint.
My days are as simple as it gets.
I peel crates of vegetables; I do basic prep. I clean.
The pay is miserable, and my ego, usually bulletproof, is shredded. In there, I am nobody and no one, so humiliations are served daily.

But I hold on. I cling to anything I can think of.
I learn a craft.
I discover humility.
Self-respect.
Pride in a job done right.
Life.
Day after day, I claw back my dignity. I rebuild myself; I resurface. I come home wrecked—but this time it's by fatigue. No Coke. A couple of drinks, sure, out of habit, but I'm done killing myself. I am done with self-destruction. Not anymore.
Because for once in my life, I am at peace.
I peeled asparagus all day and trimmed parsley, and I reek of onions, but I am excited like a kid on Christmas morning.
Because I finally belong. I've got a place.
And little by little, with hard work, I gradually earned the other cooks' respect; they accept me.
Then one day, I get my goddamned ordination.
My first jacket.
My first knife.
I am one of them. I'm in the brotherhood now.
Chef de partie. I am a cook; I have my station, my line. The right kind this time.
I am part of the tribe. And I finally can focus on my main goal:
To become the boss of this madhouse, the one commanding these maniacs armed with sharp blades.
I am not worried I'll make it happen because I stink of ambition, and my determination has no limit.

And no, it didn't happen in two seasons of Top Chef. It took years of sweat, struggle, and endless nights. Burns, doubts, perseverance. Because I didn't go to culinary school. So I had to work harder. Faster. I hustled like a madman because I knew nothing.

All those years I had to shut my mouth and climb the rungs. Secretly fuming because I am always carrying that hatred of authority like a second skin.

And I bled for it. Because kitchens aren't democracies. Nobody asks for your opinion. You do what you're told, you shut the fuck up, open your ears, grind, and become a cook.

And I swallowed it all in silence. My mistakes, the shit, my ignorance.

But I never gave up.

Never.

Till I became sous-chef.

Six months later, one evening the boss pulls me aside at closing.

"Shit, what the fuck did I do again?"

Then he drops the bomb on me:

The chef is leaving; do you want the job?

After what felt like an endless battle, I finally made it. I am a chef de cuisine.

I'll never forget that day.

I raced home; I couldn't wait to tell Peggy.

I felt like a soldier who'd crossed hell and survived.

On the drive, ♫ *Ultraviolet* by U2 exploded through the car speakers, ripping through me.
I cranked it.
It wasn't Bono I heard. It was Peggy.
Every lyric, every note, was an electric wire pulling me back to her. Her voice, her hand on my shoulder, and her eyes pushing me forward.
I thought of my wife not just like you think of someone but as a light at the end of a tunnel. A torch that's guiding you to drag you out of the darkness. A lighthouse planted in the middle of a battlefield.
She gave me the strength to climb out of the mud, to move forward, to fight.
She picked me up when I was almost damaged goods, brain-dead, hollow, and hopeless.

I owe her everything.
She owes me nothing.
We're even.
I love that woman more than my own life

As for work,
Veni, vidi, vici.
I have my name stitched on my jacket.
It's my kitchen now.
My parish.
My church

Open the gates of hell and bring me Lucifer.
I've got a few words for him.

Untitled

This feels like the right moment to take a break. Not because I'm tired. But there are a few truths that need to be said out loud. Because what comes next isn't something you just skim past.
And maybe you'll need time to digest this.
I didn't really know how to title this chapter.
I sat with it for a long time, turning it over in my head, trying to pin down a title that made sense. Something that could hold the weight of what's coming next.
Well, nothing fits.
So it'll stay untitled.
And without a song.
Why?
Because there aren't many words that can explain what follows. And the ones that exist all feel inadequate. Too soft, too clean, too distant from the reality of who I was back then.
Nothing feels sharp enough, violent enough, or precise enough to describe the failure of a man I had become.
And I refuse to stain a song with my downfall.
You don't put a soundtrack on a free fall.
No air. No poetry.
There's nothing beautiful to pull out of that moment. Just filth, shame, waste, and the slow collapse of a man who managed to sink lower than he ever thought possible.

When I first finished this book, it ended before this part. The story was complete, or at least I thought it was. But when I went back and read it again, something was missing—something ugly, something essential.

A piece of my life that I couldn't just edit out.

So I added this chapter, even though I didn't want to.

Because there's a stretch of my life that I don't get to erase, no matter how much I'd like to forget about it. Or rather, not remember it.

This is about how drugs and booze rotted me.

How I almost destroyed everything around me.

And how close I was to not coming back from the dark hole I put myself into.

I hate talking about it. And to tell you the truth, I had no intention of ever putting it on paper. Too many blackouts, too many gaps, too many memories I worked hard to bury.

But it happened.

Remember, I said at the beginning of the book: I would not sugarcoat anything.

So, here it is.

By the time my daughter was born, I was already burnt out—cocaine and vodka fried my brain. My judgment was nonexistent; whatever common sense I had left didn't last very long.

And I lost my job. Once again we found ourselves in a situation that felt painfully familiar: late rent, no plan, no way out. All because of me.

So we made a decision that, at the time, sounded like a fresh start. We left the United States and moved to Sint Maarten.
Here it comes again.
That island that I already knew too well.
An island that, in hindsight, felt more like a graveyard than a refuge.
An island of ghosts.
An island I swear today I'd never set foot on again in my life.
Too many bad memories.

We settle in a quiet neighborhood next to the beach. We move into a cute pink house with a garden and a little pool.
On paper, it looks like the perfect reset button we desperately need.
Peggy agrees to work at her parents' restaurant, stepping into something stable, something real.
I, on the other hand, am convinced, as usual, that my so-called "genius" will save me one more time, and I decide to switch sides entirely.
I tell myself I can do the job of a chef.
With no experience worth mentioning, no real foundation—just ego and delusion.
I work on my resumé, dressing it up. And when I have an interview, I sell the story the way I always have. And somehow, because I can talk my way into almost anything, I am hired as a head chef at a beach restaurant.
It didn't take long for reality to catch up.
I am clueless and completely out of my depth. I am doing crap.

No technique, no discipline, no structure.
I am improvising and calling it instinct. I am sending out plates that should never leave any kitchen.
I have the perfect recipe for a downfall, roasted and cooked by the flames of my incompetence and my arrogance.
So, as I am losing control, I work from eight to five but never sober. I am high and drunk through the service. Then I come home completely wasted, even though I am supposed to take care of my daughter while my wife takes her shift at work.

That situation lasted about a month.
I wasn't fooling anyone, least of all Peggy. She could see exactly what was going on, even when I tried to deny it.
I was spiraling—paranoid and a mythomaniac.
Full of lies and excuses, I barely believed myself.
And, unsurprisingly, I lost that job too.
That was the end of the road. At least for me.
The rope had held for as long as it could, but it was fraying, and I could feel it snapping.
My life was hanging by something so thin it barely deserved to be called a thread anymore.

One night, after a shift at another dead-end kitchen job, I get into my car completely wasted.
Two hundred meters past the restaurant, there's a turn.
I go straight off the road, right down the cliff.
The car flips over and over before finally stopping at the bottom of the ravine.

When I come back to my senses, everything is quiet.
It takes me a few seconds—maybe more—to figure out what happened, where I am, or even what direction I am facing.
The car is upside down, flat as a pancake, crushed against a tree. The trunk is pressed so close to my face I can feel it when I breathe.
I am just lying there, inverted. In every possible sense.
I crawl out through what's left of the windshield, squeezing between twisted metal and dirt. I drag myself free, grabbing my bag, which ended up right next to me.
It's pitch black: no streetlights, no noise, nothing but a very awkward silence.
I climb back up the ravine, step by step—slipping, bleeding, and pulling myself up until I reach the road again. Then I walk back to the restaurant.
My arms and legs are cut up from glass and debris, but otherwise... nothing. No broken bones. No major injuries. By a sheer miracle.
I am alive.

As I arrive at the restaurant, I ask if someone can drive me home.
On the way back, we stop down the road and grab a couple of flashlights to check what's left of that car. It is just a crushed cube of metal, plastic, and glass.
My friend looks at me, asking,
— How the fuck did you get out of this?
To tell you the truth, I shouldn't have made it out.

I shouldn't be here to write this.
Call it luck, fate, or whatever you want.
All I know is that I walked away from something that should have ended me.
To this day, I still don't know why or how.

I go home and Peggy sees me walk in like that—covered in cuts, still reeking of alcohol and stupidity.
I explain to her what happened like it was just another story, another episode in the long list of bad decisions.
She doesn't explode.
She doesn't scream or yell.
It is worse than that.
She has one of those cold angers. Silent. Internal.
The kind that doesn't fade.
She is done. Exhausted. I can feel it.

A week later, she tells me she is going to Miami for the weekend with the kids to visit friends.
Once she gets there, she calls me.
We have a short casual conversation. Like nothing happened. Then she tells me she has to go; she'll call me back tomorrow.
I know something is coming my way. There is no way I am getting out of this that easily.
The next day, she calls and drops it, like she's telling me the time of day.
Cold, ruthless.
—She is not coming back.
No drama, no negotiation. Just a clean cut.
That's it. It's over.

I am back to square one.
Alone in an empty house, surrounded by the wreckage I had created. I am following a path that suddenly looks very familiar—a lot like my father's.
And for the first time, I see it clearly: I am a failure. At everything.
I am struggling to see a way out; I am convinced there is only one thing left to do.
End it.
For two days, I drink non-stop until my liver begs for mercy while I run through my options.
What is the best way to finish it once and for all: Pills, another crash, overdose—I am only missing a gun.
The car crash didn't get me; fine, I'll do it myself.

Then a fucking miracle happens. Another one.
One week after she left, my rescue comes with a phone call. My wife tells me:
—If you want to get us back, you have to stop your bullshit.
That's it. No speech. No sugarcoating. No second chances spelled out.
Just a line in the sand.
It's that or the grave.
The next morning, I got on the first plane.

You already know what comes next.
A double espresso.
A promise.
A sentence that changes everything.
"I want to be a chef."

And I started over.

Why didn't I include this in the previous chapter? Because there's no way in hell I'd drag this shit into the one part of the book that is about the person who means everything to me.
She deserves better than this.
You might not like what I'm about to say, but here it is:
I love my daughter to death, and I'd give my life for her.
But my wife—she's my anchor, my compass, my everything. Without her, I have nothing. I'm nothing.
The rest... that's my mess, my noise.

With time and in her infinite patience and unbelievable generosity, Peggy forgave me.
But me? Hell no. I don't forgive myself. I don't give myself that luxury.
The humiliation, the damage, the pain I caused. That stays with me. It's not something I get to forget or smooth over.
I carry it. It's my burden. My responsibility.
Today, I haven't forgotten a thing, and I make damn sure I never will. It fuels me. It fuels my rage, my hate for failure, and my drive to survive.
I owe her a debt that I'll never be able to repay, because she saved my life.
I was one step away from punching my ticket, and that day, whether I deserved it or not, became the first day of the rest of my life.

You'll find out the rest of the story soon.
But it was important that you knew this. You needed to know.
It explains a lot. That's the reason for my mindset, who I am, how I think, and why I still carry certain things with me.
Alright, now we can move on.
Let's get back to the story.
But fair warning; the next chapter is the Miami massacre.
And it's just as hard to swallow.

Miami CSI

City Selling Illusions
Or
Chaos Served Indefinitely.
Both work.
Pick Your Poison!

! WARNING !

This is the first of a few chapters like this.
This chapter is crude and raw in places and unapologetically so. Some might be offended by my language.
Am I sorry? Hell no.
Because everything mentioned here is true, happened, happens, and is happening.
If it rubs you the wrong way, skip ahead—or better yet, never set foot in this dump of a city.
And if you still decide to come here anyway after reading this.
Well, you can't say I didn't warn you.

First, I need to say that I love the USA.
This country adopted me; it gave me a second carcer, and I loved every minute of the twenty years I've spent here. I owe it a lot.
I like Americans—their blind faith in their dream, their pride, and their SUV-sized innocence.
It's beautiful, inspiring, always...and overplayed... sometimes. But at least they believe in it. They charge in, head down, guns locked and loaded.
We, the French, comment on, analyze, and live in what used to be.

America reinvents herself every decade.
When I was a kid, the U.S. was my beacon, my dream, my goal.
The movies, the American way of life, Madison Square Garden, John McEnroe, Agassi, etc.
And then I went to New York; I fell in love with it the second I arrived. Because Manhattan's got a soul, a heartbeat, and a voice. It's dense, tense, organic, and juiced on pure voltage.

Unfortunately, even the best and the greatest can make mistakes, right?
And this one, America, I'll shove it right in your face.
Because Miami is a DNA glitch in the existence of this great nation. An omen, a sacrilege from a country that brought to the world so much greatness.
So don't see this as a rant; it's not against this nation or your people or even the system, but a love letter from a broken heart.
Yes, America, I have to tell you the truth: you broke my heart because you gave birth to an atrocity. And after twenty years, I just can't take it anymore. I am mentally exhausted.

So, I hope you're hungry, because as promised, the chef presents you today's special:
Roasted Miami, glazed with Guns N' Roses and a reduction of The Who.

The recipe calls for a pinch of ♫ *Won't Get Fooled Again* and a dash of ♫. *Welcome to the jungle.*

A toxic combo—the cancer and the cholera in stereo.

Why toss two songs?

Well, not like makeup and lipstick, not like perfume and fancy clothes, but more like pouring two chemicals together in a trash can to cover the stench.

I can't stand either song or either band.

Just hearing Axl Rose's nasal screech gives me the shits. It's loud, greasy, shrill, vulgar, tacky, cheap, and greasy.

Not the good kind of grease, not butter or duck fat. I'm talking rancid carnival fryer oil that's been sitting too long.

As for The Who?

I was going to make a cheap joke.

Ah, screw it.

As for The Who... well, let's just say the joke writes itself.

There, I said it.

As I have a twisted mind, I even thought of the band Garbage. It sounded promising. But I couldn't make it past the third track.

The truth is, this city practically forced those songs on me because you're trapped between blasting A/C and sticky humidity that glues your balls to your thighs, full-blown panic attacks on Xanax, and streets that reek of weed at every corner.

A jungle, which I had already been through once. And I'm not letting it fool me twice.
So yeah, those two songs fit perfectly for this place that I despise and loathe.
And mostly, because bad taste deserves its own anthem.

Miami is the American dream spray-painted in pastel and frozen in collagen.
A Telemundo soap opera with no subtitles because, here, nobody speaks English anymore.
It's not the American dream I was told about when I was a kid. And regarding that famous *American* efficiency?
Frame it, hang it in your bathroom, or flush it. It's useless here.

Forget the neon dream of *Miami Vice* reruns or Michael Mann's glossy fantasies with their dreamy skylines.
Yes, the water is turquoise. That part is real.
But the sand? Pulverized rock, bleached and spread out like makeup over something rotten.
Because underneath it all, this city is built on swamp and sludge.
Miami is a façade—everything about it engineered, polished, and fundamentally fake.
It's flash first, rot underneath.
Think of it as an aging stripper who just hit the lottery.
She got a makeover.

A full facelift, funded by billions coming from her prime position as a global hub for... powder. And it's not Tinker Bell's Pixie Dust.
She had quite a lot of work done, and now she's all plastic and lies.
Fake smile, fake tits, fake ass. Designer clothes with the brand name in your face. In a nutshell, a fancy grifter with zero class.
When she is doing her routine on you, from a distance, she glitters. She has tan skin and lust dripping from her eyes. So you get closer; then she opens her arms and invites you into a foamy Jacuzzi.
And when she's done with you, you crawl out itching, with plantar warts and a life in pieces.
Your bank account is empty; you've got nothing but debt and tears.
And when you piss, it burns.
Provocative, sure.
Cheap? Absolutely.
But you see the image, and like me, you gag.
You're nauseous; good. That's the point.
That's the whole story of this city.

Welcome to the place where plastic surgery isn't a medical secret but a national sport.
Post-op compression garments are the new uniform. No need to hide. And seeing someone in one at Starbucks is as normal as spotting a tourist in flip-flops.
Around here, scars are war medals.
Thanks to the BBL, the liposuction three-sixty combo, and the Brazilian butt lift, the city is

packed with clones and frozen smiles. And if you don't have an hourglass figure that bends the laws of physics, good luck convincing anyone you actually live here.
And with an average annual daytime temperature of eighty-four degrees Fahrenheit all year round, the "natural body" has become a vintage option.
The pressure is so intense you start wondering if implants come included with the lease.
People don't save for retirement; they save for their next facelift.
What's the point of having money at eighty if you don't look thirty on Instagram today?
Long story short: Miami is probably the only place on earth where plastic is more biodegradable than human relationships.

Each neighborhood has its own aesthetic "vibe" and deeply rooted stereotypes:
South Beach is the temple of bling.
The highest concentration of inflatable dolls you'll ever see. Maximum look: radioactive tans and gravity-defying bodies. If your lips don't take up thirty percent of your face, you're probably a lost tourist.
Brickell is the Wall Street aesthetic.
The stereotype? Invisible maintenance.
Nobody gets surgery; they just "rejuvenate" (after five thousand dollars of Botox and fillers). The goal is to look like a crypto trader who has never experienced any stress.
Coral Gables is old money.

It's the cosmetic surgery aristocracy with royal high-end clinics everywhere.
The look is “generational wealth”: facelifts so perfect they pass for good genetics since the sixties. It’s where you go to get “adjusted” without the country club neighbors noticing.
Wynwood? That’s “Artsy Plastic.”
Even surgery has to look indie.
You’ll see people covered in tattoos with laser-perfect skin. It’s the only place where you can debate contemporary art while comparing jawline injections.

Wait, I’m not done. Let’s not forget the “forever young” dudes. No sexism here.
Because the new male trend is the “natural look” that contains more silicone and CO_2 lasers than actual DNA.
Why bother with a gym membership when you can pay a guy in Coral Gables to vacuum your dad bod and carve abs straight into your skin?
That’s the ultimate Miami dream: spend six weeks in a compression suit just to end up looking like an action figure left too close to a radiator.
And between chin implants sharp enough to cut glass and “Daddy Do-Overs,” local guys are one surgery away from being more aerodynamic than a Gulf-stream jet.
But hey, who needs to blink or move their forehead when the jaw does all the work?
Because behind those marble-white veneers, you can almost hear them mumble:
“I own a yacht I absolutely cannot afford.”

That's the local wildlife and its customs.

Apparently, that's still not enough to scare people off. And every year, more suckers show up to settle in this rat hole.
Rats that, by the way, also have Instagram accounts.
As for the cockroaches... they're freelance.
You think I'm vulgar?
Too aggressive?
Over the top?
Let me tell you what life in Miami really looks like. The day-to-day operations, if I may say so. Because it's the same mess everywhere, including the restaurant scene.

When I first landed twenty years ago, there were still Cuban cafés and a couple of seafood shacks—not great, but honest.
A dusty French touch that felt dated but sincere, and a few steakhouses for bloated golfers with cigars.
Back then, the city shut down in the summer, hibernating under the sun.
It was authentic, and it had charm.
Now?
Empty skyscrapers sprouting everywhere like bad weeds and endless traffic jams.
And for the last five years, the restaurant scene has been on crack. The number of restaurants shot up seventy-four percent.
A tsunami of mediocrity.

Everyone opened their concept: the bartender, the DJ, the coked-up trader, and even the useless brainwashed influencer who discovered gnocchi three weeks ago.
Half of the places are dead within a year.
Three years? Only a quarter survives.
Five years? You're entering into unicorn territory, pure science fiction.

It's the era of phony fusions: "Sushi Burrito" or "Pizza Pasta."
Yes, you read that right.
Omakase.
Omaka-what? Don't ask me; I still haven't figured out what the hell that is.
Modern, overpriced Latin fusion and average Italians are everywhere; you can add the carbon-copy "concepts" cloned to death.
Fine dining? Extinct and buried next to white tablecloths and respect.
French cuisine? Politely but surely pushed off the radar.
As for plant-based?
It's not a trend anymore; it's the law. A must.
Yuck.
As for the over-themed restaurants serving tasteless and soulless food, they are legion. They are all promoting on Instagram the same twenty-five-dollar cocktail being served to a botoxed bimbo in a miniskirt and a plastic rack.
And nobody gives a fuck, because here you can serve crap as long as it's lit right and looks good on social networks.

To be blunt, honest cuisine is dead and buried.

As for rents? Astronomical.
Customers? Flaky. You've got one minute of attention, max.
Want to open and launch today?
Budget: three hundred thousand to two million dollars. Minimum.
And they keep opening because the city keeps growing like a tumor. Bloating would be more accurate.
It's a global buffet juiced with investment fumes and crooked investors and the illusion of good taste.
One-million-dollar concepts that die in six months without ever serving a single customer.
All this, financed by pastel-shirt dudes with too much cash and no clue.
Welcome to the burrata-laundromat capital of the world, a fiscal operation bleached with a side of truffle oil.
Your project here isn't a restaurant; it's a washing machine. Throw in dirty money; open, wash, spin, rinse, dry, close, and disappear. And repeat.
Nobody cooks. Everybody counts.

Staff?
Ghosts.
Since Covid, no one wants to get screamed at for eighteen dollars an hour. The ones who still show up are either high on Adderall or under deportation threat.
Us in the kitchen?

Underpaid, overworked, and wrung out like sponges.
Then comes the knockout punch:

Money?
Groups are buying up entire blocks. Brickell, the Design District, and Coconut Grove—all turned into Dubai suburbs on Prozac.
Glossy concepts, massive budgets, marketing armies. And a horde of consultants debating and picking the color of the toilet paper.
One giant gourmet scam run by amateurs
Small guys die; big guys get fatter.
Behind the facade? Debt, stress, burnout.
Because passion isn't enough anymore.
Bring more than a dream—you need cash, a PR firm, and a damn good shark lawyer.

And then there's life.
Or let's say what's left of it when seventy percent of your paycheck goes into rent for a LEGO-made condo.
The cost of living increased one hundred and thirty-six percent in fourteen years. Inflation is nonstop, but wages are stagnant.
Not a dream, a joke.
Rents? Insane.
A studio is about two thousand five hundred.
Two bedrooms for four thousand.
Three bedrooms: six thousand.
If you're "lucky," your neighbor's cooking meth in his bathtub, and you're woken at six a.m. by S.W.A.T. kicking his door.

Well, at least you have your something for free... the wake-up call.
Shootouts and junkies swan-diving out windows after a bad trip—it's routine.
And this is in a "nice" neighborhood.

Food?
Forget it if you don't want to live on burgers or tacos without breaking the bank or maxing out your credit card.
And you feel like buying French products; good luck.
The camembert is twenty dollars.
Saucisson, twenty-five.
Baguette? Rare, overpriced, wrapped in plastic, limp. And it tastes like shit.
But hey, you can fold it in your bag without breaking it.
Handy, right?

And when the sun sets, it's the Wild West.
I live fourteen blocks from the restaurant, which means a twenty-minute walk. That is my daytime therapy. I love it.
Nighttime? You're on edge.
You cross cracked-out junkies ready to mug you for your AirPods, hobos, drunk drivers throwing beer cans, and creeps pulling over to jerk off at stoplights.
So, I carry a Taurus. Not the fucking car, morons... the gun. I got my concealed carry permit.

When I walk the dog out with my kid at night, I've got the piece tucked under my T-shirt. But it is still not enough to make me feel safe.
Last week, in South Beach, two drivers argued over a parking spot. Mom gets two bullets in the head.
Yesterday, two blocks from the restaurant, there was an argument outside a joint, and six people were shot dead.
And here's the cherry on top:

Don't get sick.
It's cheaper and safer to die than to get treated.
Health insurance? For a family, it's six hundred a month, minimum.
Obamacare? My ass. Obama doesn't "care."
Want to see a doctor? Bring your credit card.
Appointments? Two months' wait, if you're lucky.
ER visit? One thousand dollars and a nice chance of dying in the waiting room because the doctor is clueless or worse, an idiot.
Once in the E.R., a doc asked if I'd taken any meds.
I said, "An Advil."
He said, "Never heard of it. What's that?"

That is just the beginning;
I have prepared you a little assortment of my adventures in the Miami health care system.
A medical "best of," if you want.
I picked the most spectacular. If I had to list them all, I could have written a whole book just on MDs' and hospitals' fuck-ups.

During Peggy's pregnancy, after a couple of exams, an MD comes to me, saying—no, let's be fair—screaming that she has cancer and she needs surgery today. Insisting he can't save both. So, I need to choose between my wife or the kid.
And I have to make my mind fast.
I try to stay cool, and I demand a second opinion.
In the same hospital, mind you.
Because you never know?
After a sleepless night, the next morning, the new doc—after looking at the exact same scans—comes to me and let me know his findings.
Guess what?
No cancer.
Both are fine.
Thanks for the trauma, doc.

When my daughter was born, her coccyx was red and sticking out. Diagnosis from the pediatrician:
—She's going to have a tail.
My wife and I looked at each other, and I landed a joke.
— Like a dog?
Doctor, dead serious:
—Yes. Exactly.

A few months later, her skull was misshapen, and at every visit, the pediatrician—not the same one —mocked her. kept calling her the "Flat Head Princess."
I guess we're not fond of her sense of humor, to say the least.

Peggy did her own research.
Turns out it was plagiocephaly. Her skull is growing only on one side, while her brain is still expanding.
Serious condition. Urgent treatment.
Resin helmet for two years.
That idiot hadn't noticed a thing.
Trust me, you don't want to see the bill.

Speaking of which, writing this reminds me I still owe my half-sister money. Yeah, my mom's daughter.
When my kid's treatment cost eighteen thousand dollars and we were flat broke. So, we asked for a little help from friends.
Turns out she found out, and she sent me twenty bucks. Yes, twenty.
I should thank her someday.
Well, I'm sure we'll cross paths again.
Justine, when that happens, run.
Fast.

Where was I? Oh yeah.
Then came the broken arm.
Rafaelle needed a metal rod in her elbow.
Four thousand dollars for the operation. Six hundred and twenty dollars for the ambulance ride. And a nurse who jabbed her fourteen times before finding a vein right before surgery.

And me?
Twelve years ago, I had a sore throat.

After some tests, they told me it was throat cancer.
And I had three or four months to live.
Guess what? I'm still here.
Never went back to a doctor since.
Truth? I'm done with those clowns.

I'm running on fumes because everything here is violent. Werther Moral. Physical. Medical or financial.
And as for the Floridian Mirage?
Work, survive, bleed, and pay with a smile, or you're out.
At work, you're not a human being; you're a spreadsheet line. And once you're useless, they toss you out like a washed-up quarterback.
No warning, no second chances.
Especially at our age.
Especially in the restaurant industry.
Especially in kitchens.

But here's why New York is the exact opposite.
There is no Botox and neon, but blood and steel.
Not hypocritical smiles, but clenched jaws.
Not swamp heat, but subway steam blasting your face at two a.m.
New York is beautiful and majestic.
Brutal and wired on adrenaline.
New York doesn't seduce you; it grabs you by the balls.
You earn your place, or you get chewed up. There is no middle ground.
Where Miami is a fantasy, New York is a scar.

It hurts, but it's real.
Every block is sweat, ambition, and drama.
Every corner smells like a different kitchen, a different dream, a different downfall.
That's my America.
That's my home away from home.
The only city I could live in away from my country.
It's the mothership far from the motherland.
Not the stripper with fake tits but the fighter with broken teeth who still stands tall.
Funny how two cities brought such different fates.
New York made me feel alive; it gave me the fire.
Miami drained me, drowned my illusions, and wiped out every hope.
I could talk about New York for hours.
You know what?
Further in the book I will write something about it.
This city deserves and will have its love letter.

So, what now?
The only thing I know is I want to get the fuck out of here, but to go where?
It's funny how every chapter of my life is a different city. Paris, New York, London, St. Barth, and now Miami.
So maybe it's time to write a new one.
Not today, but tomorrow.
Maybe I'll tell you the story the day after.
I am going to give you a hint—it's going to be a tale of two, or maybe three.

The three horsemen of the apocalypse

Now that I've wrecked the mood with my chainsaw-shaped life story and the Miami clusterfuck, let's move on to something more cheerful.
Or at least something more honest and decent.

Go on, don't hover by the door. Step inside.
I know you've always wondered what really happens behind those padded doors. And what gets said when the tickets start piling up and the dining room fills.
Well, here, take a jacket and stand next to me.
Just understand one thing before we begin:
This isn't a show. It's going to get loud, hot, and a little ugly.

Like I said before, those fine-dining kitchens with morgue lighting, hospital vibes, Napoleonic hierarchy, and a kitchen brigade hooked on Xanax. Not my scene. No, thanks.
I'd rather roll with a tight crew.
A sous-chef riding the grill. One guy on sides and fryers, another juggling starters and desserts, and me at the pass, working the sauté and calling the shots. It's cramped like trench warfare; it's alive, and it runs on noise and sweat. Orders fly, tempers flare, and somehow, plates keep landing where and when they're supposed to.
Most of the year, it works. Not always perfectly, but well enough.

But three times a year that balance turns straight into a multi-car pileup.
A crash. A real one.
People drunk at the wheel, flooring it at a hundred and twenty miles an hour without airbags or seatbelts.
That's what those three services feel like.
Cursed days that every cook on earth dreads and would rather get a molar ripped out with a drill than show up to work.

Got an idea?
Nope, wrong guess.
It's not New Year's Eve.
That one is just long and boring, packed with shiny couples, satin dresses, glitter jackets, fixed menus, and cheap bubbles at midnight.
It's predictable. Tedious but no surprises.
Like a funeral.
You know it's going to drag, but at least the program's printed.

The other three?
It's a whole different story. No script. No mercy.
That's when you dive headfirst into pure chaos.
An industrial torture without compassion or lube.
A one-way ticket straight into the guts of hell.
Hell, whose parade marches to the sound of ♫ *Sympathy for the Devil*. Yeah, the Stones again.
That slithering beat is like a warning coming from somewhere you shouldn't go.
The rhythm builds, the heat rises, and Jagger slides in, smooth and slow. He introduces the

Devil like he's serving a fine wine, dripping with vice.
The tension climbs, and Richards slices in with that sharp, greasy riff. It enters your soul like a hot knife through butter.
It's exactly the fuel you need to survive what's coming.
So, feel free to let go of the wheel, and when you see the wall... hit the gas.
You can honk if you want.

Alright, strap in and hold on tight; I'm going to tell you about a real trauma. The kind that brands your brain with insomnia and wakes you up drenched in sweat, heart pounding like a war drum, brain fried like a forgotten pan on full blast. And mentally sane only by sheer miracle. A freaky, greasy, heavy nightmare that sticks to your soul and leaves you kneeling in the walk-in fridge. Hands shaking and staring at the frozen shrimp, hoping they will answer your prayers. Because every year, those three services get worse.
More people, less logic. But all one at a time.
So what could give you hives or trigger a panic attack just hearing its name?
I'll tell you.
Please meet the unholy trio.
Let me introduce you to what I like to call the three horsemen of the Apocalypse.
Not because it's poetic, but because it feels accurate.
Beelzebub, Satan, and Lucifer.

All clocked in, aprons on, knives sharpened, ready to carve your soul.
We will forget for now Cupid and his arrow up his ass, and Mommy's Day of glory—that circus will come later. At least they only show up once a year.
Let's focus on the first one.
This motherfucker rides in fifty-two times a year.
Yeah, fifty-two.
A cosmic turd, a weekly recycled torture.
The divine punishment for every sin committed in a kitchen.

Spoiler:
It's Sunday.
It smells like scrambled eggs, frying oil, and steamed-milk foam.

Purgatory, with kids screaming in the background.
Dante's Inferno, served with hollandaise.

Brunch

Black mass, hell on a plate

The first horseman has arrived.
Not on a stallion, but in neon jogging pants.
Stroller in tow, rolling in with his whole crew and
a reservation at eleven thirty a.m. sharp.

Brunch, to me, has never been a meal. It's not a
trend, not even a phase. But more like a pathogen.
A recurring infection that keeps mutating and
coming back stronger every Sunday.
A full-blown war against common sense and
sanity.
A sacrificial ritual built on pancakes, burgers, and
cappuccinos.
I wouldn't call it a catastrophe—more like a
calamity of biblical proportions. Like the plague.
On Sunday God rested, but we?
We got crucified.

This idiotic invention, this bastard child of
breakfast and lunch, has infected the entire
industry.
An abomination imagined by some soulless
sociopath. And to this degenerate who spawned
this idea, I wish him a slow, long, filthy, and
agonizing death. May you rot in hell and be
haunted for eternity by the demons you unleashed
in our kitchen and on us, poor suckers in white
jackets.

With time, brunch has become an urban guerrilla disguised as a lazy Sunday. A sacred massacre served at the same time every week.

My own ♫ *Sunday Bloody Sunday*.

Unlike U2, we're not talking about blood here. But lukewarm milk, bacon torched to ash, and orange juice bleeding out like a collective hemorrhage.
No bullets here, just "special requests."
The casualties?
Us.
The executioners?
Couples in shorts demanding vegan, gluten-free waffles "that somehow still taste like childhood nostalgia.

Let's rewind and set the scene, because context matters.
I'm a born-and-bred Parisian, raised on tight, stylish restaurants that had structure, rhythm, and a kind of elegance. You worked hard for lunch and dinner. But nothing in between. Except for some time to reset. There was logic to it.
You sent clean plates. You fired off your tuna tataki or your filet mignon to the soundtrack of "the best of lounge music" or "chill house greatest hits."
Groovy. Punchy. Funky.
Back then, in Paris, brunch was barely a thing. A niche habit. I saw it as a hangover cure for hipster zombies crawling out from famous nightclubs like Les *Bains Douches or Chez Castel.*

Even as a customer, I wanted to blow my brains out when I was asked to come to brunch.
I always had the same answer.
—No. Go to hell with your brunch. I want a croissant, a baguette with butter and jam, and a coffee—like a functioning adult. Leave me the fuck alone with your Benedict eggs, avocado toasts, and your lukewarm mimosas.

But when you work in the U.S.,
Brunch isn't optional. It's institutional. Industrial. You can run, but you can't hide. And it will find you, drag you in, and make you pay. So this nightmare is a non-negotiable diet. You swallow it till you choke.
First, as a dining room manager, I witnessed, helpless, all logic collapse.
Later, when I crossed over into the kitchen, I landed in another dimension—a dark, unfathomable one, a bottomless pit ruled by demons in flip-flops and couples in yoga pants whispering.
— We'd like something light and low-carb.
But this time I wasn't just watching the slaughter.
I was the conductor of the goddamned orchestra.
That's when I learned what pain really means.
I felt it in my bones.
And believe me, that was just the beginning.

My first brunch service in an American restaurant is burned into me like a cattle brand. I honestly thought I'd croak on the spot.

That day, the printer was possessed by the devil. Vomiting endless tickets with modifiers stacked on more modifiers until it barely resembled English.
Only one burger on the menu.
One.
And I cranked out eighty of them.
I swear: EIGHTY.
I was convinced the servers had some secret menu they were sliding under the table, with nothing on it but that piece of crap. Just to piss me off.
Traitors. Judas rats. May you all scorch in the oil of the deep fryer.
Yes, I know I am about to commit the ultimate sacrilege, but here, have it:
I can't stomach burgers; eating or cooking them bores me to death.
A sad slab of ground beef trapped between two sweaty slices of bread, with fifty Lego-block modifications:
With cheese, no cheese, Swiss, American, or cheddar.
Pickles, no pickles.
Grilled onions, raw onions, caramelized onions.
Tomato, no tomato, or sun-dried tomato.
— I'll have the burger with no bun, no sauce, no meat... just a lettuce leaf and the ghost of a pickle.
Five people, five different burgers.
What the hell?

And the eggs.

Scrambled, runny, poached, flipped, fried, soft-boiled, or omelet half-cooked but runny—but not too much.
—Can I have a fried sunny-side egg but just the yolk? (Yes, that happened.)
They want a ray of sunshine, no sky, no clouds.
Just the essence of the egg.
What's next, a coffee with no cup?
Are you kidding me?

And then, of course, my favorite, the holy grail of bullshit:
The egg-white omelet.
Always off-menu, but there's always one dumbass to order it. And usually the herd follows.
—Oh yeah, me too. So healthy!
Yeah, sure, it'll go great with your plate of fries drowning in ketchup, the six sodas, the fourteen pancakes, and the gallon of maple syrup you just wolfed down.
Knowing that, imagine the poor server who walks in the kitchen. He approaches the pass slowly and carefully, like he's walking into a minefield.
The guy's already trembling because he knows what happened a week ago. He remembers the guy who got yelled at for sending a ticket with a burger rare inside and well-done outside. (Yeah, that actually happened too).
He shuffles in, pale as milk, eyes pleading like my dog when he smells beef.
—Chef... uh... egg-white omelet... Hmm?
I stare at him.

He starts melting in his shirt, about to shit himself
I breathe, grind my teeth... and nod with a smirk.
What do you want me to do or say?
It's not his fault. It's the clients. These rabid, capricious trolls in sneakers and sweatpants.
I am not going to shred him.
Not yet.
But his time will come.
He'll pay for his betrayal in due time.

I am joking. Well, kind of.
I have eternal respect for the front-of-house staff.
I've been there; I sweated with them.
I served hordes of hysterical moms in Lululemon with kids licking the table and grandmas demanding their mimosas with organic orange juice squeezed by elves, with some pulp but not too much.
Oh yes, I remember you, evil clients.
I smiled through your requests that should be classified as crimes against common sense.
Treating staff like punching bags, dropping gems like
—Your ice cubes aren't cold enough. (True story.)
Or the hotshot showing off for his date but not knowing jack:
—I'd like a red Sauvignon. What do you recommend? (Also, true.)
A what? I recommend you shut the fuck up.
Anyway.

That day, I finished service like a KO'd boxer. Brain scrambled like fucking eggs and body ground to pulp like a damn burger patty.

Every brunch, it's the same clusterfuck in every restaurant on earth.
We know; we talk to each other.
If one day you're around at a table of chefs talking about brunch, sit down and listen. You'll pee in your pants.
The only thing is that adrenaline? It's a drug.
You spit on it, cry about it, and curse it. But you come crawling back.
Saturday night, when they check the schedule and their stomachs drop.
—Do I have brunch tomorrow?
But if you're off, you miss it.
Because you want to dive back into the huddle and get chewed up all over again.
Usually on Sunday night, when the dust settles after the army of starving zombies storms out, it's like crawling out of a nuclear hangover.
You're still standing, but you feel like you're in the twilight zone.

I remember one day, after service, we gathered to regroup. To take a breath.
I saw the boss walking into the kitchen. I was surprised because he usually never showed up on Sundays. But that afternoon he was on the verge of a breakdown. He was covered in milk stains, with cinnamon stuck in his hair.

I’m guessing he got drafted by the floor manager and spent the day churning out the one hundred and fifty cappuccinos we served that day.
He gave me the death glare, the “don’t talk to me” look.
Our eyes met.
As I couldn't help myself, I cracked a joke.
— Hey boss, do you want a latte?
We burst out laughing, and then he waved me out front.
As I stepped into his dining room, I saw that his beautiful modern-pop-culture-vibe dining room was gone. What was left looks like a war zone. Corpses of fries and gnawed waffle stumps smeared across the battlefield. And crushed berries on his expensively designed white banquettes.
He stared at me asked,
—Is it like this every Sunday?
I answer.
—This? This is nothing. Come next week; it is going to be worse.
It’s the ultimate slaughter.
A nuclear blast.
It’s Mother’s Day.

Mother's Day

Family neuroses and culinary FUBAR

The second horseman doesn't show up in armor. She walks in wearing a floral dress, bathed in an organic and ethical trade channel's vanilla fragrance. Followed by a husband who already regrets the reservation, two kids hanging off her arms, and an extended, blended family trailing behind like a slow-moving parade. With a reservation for twelve people at noon sharp.
Of course.

This day is not a celebration but a trap.
What looks, from the outside, like a warm, sentimental ritual quickly turns into a full-scale disaster—a cataclysm of waffles, made-to-order omelets, and decades of unresolved family tension. All served with a polite smile
And me?
I am in the kitchen, kneeling at the altar of chaos. Because every plate is a minefield, every customer is a ticking time bomb.
Every table is a potential incident.
Every order is a negotiation.
Every screaming kid is a shrill cry ripping away the last shred of my sanity.

And in the back of my mind, I hear ♫ *Mama* playing on loop. Phil Collins is shouting with that greasy, deranged, sardonic laugh echoing through the noise. As if even he understands that something has gone deeply wrong here. He

sounds just as messed up as me. And deep inside I'm not even sure if he's looking for his mom or laughing at me.
He's howling in despair, like I scream from frustration. He"s pounding the drums the same way this day is beating the shit out of me.
He's crying for his mother, and we, in the kitchen, are praying ours isn't anywhere near here.

This Sunday morning, you wake up already tense with a metallic taste in your mouth; your body is stiff, and your brain is already screaming for mercy.
— Today is Mother's Day, baby; get ready to suffer.
It's brunch again. Yeah, nothing new there. Except this one's spiked with nuclear drama and seasoned with every culinary meltdown and family anxiety known to humankind.
You walk into the kitchen at seven a.m.; the sun is shining outside, and birds are chirping.
But it is the calm before the storm, and the smell of chaos is brewing in the air. It's going to be rough. There's going to be meat on the walls and blood on the tiles.
An hour later, you are already all drenched in sweat, cracking open cases of eggs, tearing through stacks of English muffins, and prepping Canadian bacon like you're stocking up for a siege.
You check your mise en place twice, maybe three times, and say a small prayer. Not for success, just

for survival and for the fryer not to die mid-service. because if it does, you're fucked.
Like a week ago.

And of course, there's the "Special Mother's Day Menu."
A brain fart.
A fine piece of bullshit imagined by some marketing genius who doesn't know how to poach an egg but has talent for poetic names:
—Tenderness Toast.
Which will be requested crispy but not too crispy, grilled only on one side, warm but not dry, and topped with a perfectly ripe avocado.
Except the avocados are hard as rocks.
The supplier screwed me.
That bastard. I'll find him after service... with dirty and dull knives. So even if I don't finish him off, the infection will.
— Happiness Omelet.
Which will be ordered in one hundred different versions with twenty-eight modifications each.
— Benedict of Love.
That will be two hundred poached eggs fired à la minute and hollandaise that will break every thirty minutes because the kitchen is hotter than Satan's sauna.
— Fluffy Pancakes of Joy.
Those soft, fluffy lies stick stubbornly to the griddle like they've decided to die there. The only way to scrape them off will be with a spatula or a stick of dynamite.

— Crème brûlée with a corny flavor and a macaron on top.
Which means some pain in the ass will ask for "just a plate of macarons to share," and of course, you've got exactly the right count for dessert service.

So the madness begins, and it kicks off at eleven sharp.
The first wave of maniacs crashes in.
Mom, Dad, and the half-deaf Grandma, who forgot her glasses. By the way, she can't hear a thing, and she can't read shit... so taking the order is going to be a ball.
The annoying sister-in-law nobody can stand.
The sulking son-in-law who checked out emotionally somewhere around the parking lot.
The spoiled kids who are glued to their iPads and a stroller the size of a tank parked right in the middle of the aisle.
Hell, maybe even a dog, too.
Wait! Is it a golden retriever or a lab?
Then, it's VIP treatment.
Just like in my house. Rocky, my golden, is the king of the castle. He'll get his plate and will be served before anyone else.
My kitchen, my rules. Fuck you very much.

Orders start coming in, and none of them make sense. They all want something different: hot, fast, and with a smile.
— A white omelet with a poached yolk on top, no fat.

Huh? What the hell do you want, you psycho?
— A crispy vegan waffle with sugar on the side?
Sure, sweetheart.
— Kids want well-done burgers with ketchup but no pickles, no bun, and American cheese... and another slice of cheese unmelted on the side and fries, no salt, extra crispy but not dry.
Basically, a puzzle of culinary stupidity.
You have to be kidding me.

And Mom—oh—Mom's the queen today.
Her day, her rules.
She wants to treat herself.
She wants something sweet, but not too sweet.
Savory, but not too salty.
Light, but indulgent.
Decadent but not fat.
Gourmet, but casual.
Not too greasy, chef, but rich, you know?
Something refined but not intimidating.
Healthy, but comforting.
Basically, she wants a freaking unicorn on a plate.
What the hell do you want, lady?
An orgasm made of quinoa.
You want a pedicure too while you eat, princess?
You don't want a meal; you want therapy.
You don't need a menu; you need a shrink.
And of course, she says it with that self-satisfied smile, like the world revolves around her omelet.
Meanwhile, you're back here juggling molten pans and hollandaise grenades, wondering if you should just serve her a candle and a Xanax.

Behind the pass, you watch the world collapsing as tickets are piling up like a landslide. You are screaming, sweating, losing years of your life minute by minute; your hands are full of blisters, and your apron is painted with egg.
The commis look at you like rabbits on Vicodin.
The sous-chef panics; there is no more bacon. So you send someone running to the corner store.
The oven burns a batch of pies; the dish pit is underwater...
And the dining room is still filling up.

In the end, the service lasts three and a half hours of nonstop carnage. total suffering.
You sent two hundred eggs, ten liters of hollandaise, thirty-eight failed pancakes, nineteen complaints, three burnouts, and at least one existential crisis.
By the time you stagger out, you are a wreck.
Right when the manager barges into the kitchen when it's finished:
— Great job, chef; the clients are happy. Bravo.
You answer.
— Cool. Can I shoot myself now?

You stumble out of the kitchen like a dirty rag.
Jacket ruined, skin scorched, and soul stripped.
You haven't eaten or peed in six hours, but you're still breathing.
You have survived. But barely.
You chug three liters of water because you are dehydrated and choke down a plate abandoned

on the pass an hour ago. It's cold, sad, on its last legs, and at the end of its rope.
Just like you.
You smoke a cigarette and try to reboot your brain and process what just happened
You're fried. It was tense, and you're in shock.
It feels like you took a high-speed train in the face.

This Sunday is the ritual dismemberment of every kitchen crew. An orgy of impossible demands and servers about to be strapped into straitjackets.
And guess what?
Next year, we'll do it again.
We go back because we're masochists.
Because you're a chef, a sous, or a line cook.
Because even if we get scorched in this fire, we live for this madness, for this inferno.

We look at each other.
Guys, it's five o'clock; time to move.
It's time to clean the crime scene.
We change our apron, clean our knives, reset our station, and have fresh mise en place.

And here we go again.
Time to dive back in.
Dinner service starts in an hour.
Let's rock and roll.
You have to be fucking insane, really.

Valentine's day

Cupid can go fuck himself!

And here comes the third horseman.
But not on a white stallion.
He's strolling in like he owns the place. He's dressed up in a red tie, arms loaded with flowers, wearing that vacant, blissfully stupid smile of a man who thinks he's about to have a meaningful evening.

After the weekly brunch that wrecks your liver and fries your nerves, here comes February the fourteenth, which shows up like a final insult.
Cupid's day, Visa Platinum edition.
The reign of mercantilism, online reservations, and overpriced "romantic surprises" nobody in their right mind wants to eat.
This cursed date when love becomes a weapon of mass destruction. The only night of the year when industrial romance stomps your skull flat.

For the average customer, it's velvet hearts and roses for your sweetheart. A table for two, a pre-fixe "Elegance & Passion" menu, served on a white tablecloth sprinkled with wilted rose petals. And lit by a fake candle that probably comes from IKEA.
But for us, in the kitchen, it's blood, sweat, and bullshit.

Because behind every "I love you" scribbled in raspberry coulis, there's a kitchen on its last breath, in cardiac arrest.
Cooks on the verge of collapse, servers about to faint, twitching like junkies.
And a chef clenching his teeth, thanking whoever is up there at the moment that this Hallmark apocalypse only strikes once a year.

And always it kicks off with the same shitty soundtrack:
♫ *Endless Love* by Diana Ross & Lionel Richie.
Just the title makes you want to puke in a heart-shaped bucket.
You hear that avalanche of sugar, that lukewarm syrup of schmaltz poured by the ladle into every dining room on the planet during Valentine's Night.
I swear, you better not be diabetic.
Two voices crooning in falsetto like soggy mops dipped in marshmallow.
A slow dance for washed-up couples pretending they're still in love over a gluten-free chocolate lava cake.
The perfect soundtrack for this sentimental masquerade: a candlelight dinner with a side of shame.
A battlefield paved with crème brûlée shrapnel.
With selfies so cringe they could curdle milk and engagement promises that sound hollower than a cheap saucepan.

And guess who takes it all up the ass?

Us.
While Diana and Lionel are rubbing each other and whispering their eternal devotion, we're drowning under a tidal wave of tickets, "special requests," and hormone-crazed customers who think a ninety-dollar set menu will buy them salvation.
As for us poor bastards, who are sweating behind the pass and working that evening, it isn't the "celebration of love."
It's *Saw*, fine-dining-chaos edition.
So endless love?
Yeah.
But with stilettos in the deep fryer and blood in the whipped cream.

Let's rewind a bit.
Valentine's Day starts three weeks before at ten a.m. The phone won't stop ringing, like a car alarm drilling into your skull.
Customers are calling to book a table for two at eight p.m. by the window if possible. And to make sure the dishes will be "appropriate" for that night, you know, garlic-free, onion-free, and pleasure-free.
Sure, sir, coming right up, sir.
Yes, Madam, with pleasure, Madam.

And then there's the "special" Valentine's menu.
A monster straight out of a post-hangover nightmare.
A Frankenstein stitched together by the boss, the manager, and the chef, usually after too much

Chardonnay and not enough sleep. I've lived through it, cigarette in one hand and a bottle in the other. Yes, back when you could still smoke in restaurants... And on planes. Good old cancer-friendly days.
Anyway, that day, I asked to see the menus from previous years. just to try something different. Two years back, the chef had gone full lyrical poetry bullshit. Weirdly enough, the next year he came back to basics. Simple, elegant, effective.
Since it's my first Valentine's in this restaurant as a chef, and I've got a big mouth, balls, zero sense of self-preservation, and an ego only rivaled by my own stupidity... I want to show off.
I start pitching dishes like I'm casting spells.
—Yeah, what if we do this? And that? Oh, great, brilliant idea.
I shoot for the stars.
What I don't know yet, but will learn very quickly, is that there's not much oxygen up there.

Two days later, I do my recipes.
I plate appetizers, mains, and desserts alone in my kitchen between services. It's quiet, and I am taking my sweet time.
It looks good. It tastes good. It hits.
I bring the plates out.
We taste.
We approve.
When I am back in the kitchen, the sous-chef looks at me, eyebrows raised:
— Chef... Are you sure?

As I beam confidence, the kind only idiots have, I smile, full of swagger. And I tell him not to worry. He still stares at me and admires my nerve. But I catch a flicker of doubt.
So, to prove him wrong, I decide to push the dishes on Saturday night as specials.

Saturday, eight pm, the service starts to rock, and the more "specials" flood in, the more plates tank. Because I have no time to finesse them.
It blows up in my face in atomic proportion; from the Valentine's feast, it turns into the Valentine's Day massacre.
It's a shipwreck, and I finish service in a daze.
Bruised but not sunk, I stagger to the hostess stand, thinking we did at least one hundred fifty covers.
Nope. Ninety.
I ask how many bookings there are for Valentine's.
She drops.
— About one hundred and seventy, and still climbing.
Ouch...

The next morning, it's DEFCON ONE.
So we call an emergency summit.
The boss, the manager, and I regroup at a table again.
But this time in the morning, no smokes, no booze, just water and panic.
We agree to rebuild the menu at light speed to dodge disaster.

We strip it down. Classics only. Simple and effective. Safe and boring.
Because either way, they tell me, it's going to be FUBAR.
So:
— Amuse-bouche: Wannabe-erotic beet and goat cheese mousse.
— Appetizers: Scallop Carpaccio (frozen; of course, the good ones are already sold out).
—Main: Passion beef tenderloin with reduced jus (cooked ten different ways for ten people at the same table).

Quick detour on steak doneness—it's worth the trip.
Back home, I knew black-and-blue, rare, medium, and well-done. Simple
In the US, I've learned you guys crank it up just for sport.
Black & Blue, Rare, Medium Rare, Pittsburgh, Medium, Medium-Well, and Well Done.
And then the kicker:
Servers can scribble a "+" or "–," like it's calculus.
So sometimes you end up with "rare plus" or "medium minus."
What the fuck is medium minus?
Medium but shy?
Rare but ambitious?
Cosmic-level bullshit.
That's not cooking anymore; that's faith healing.
We're not in a kitchen anymore; we're at Lourdes.
It's not a steak; it's a goddamn miracle.

And finally, the dessert:
A molten chocolate heart... or not so molten.
Depends on whether the cook screws the timing and yanks it too early or too late.
Too runny, and it's edible diarrhea; it floods.
Too firm, you serve a hockey puck; it's as dry as divorce court.
Either way, romance is dead; like the couple's relationship, really.

Alright... Game day.
So begins the slaughter. We head into Valentine's armed to the teeth. Service starts, and tickets are raining: two-tops everywhere in endless variations.
The same shit, but never the same.
— The gentleman wants his steak somewhere between black and blue and rare, but no blood.
Seriously? Go eat tofu.
And the last-minute bombs:
— A pregnant lady requests rolls; she wants a meal with no cheese, no fish, no meat, and extra boiled veggies; no salt; no butter; just a dash of olive oil, but only if it's the cold-pressed kind.
—Anything for her?
—Yeah, here's a napkin; tell her to chew on it while I call her a cab and send her home with a bowl of rice.
Then between courses, a panicked server bursts in, sweating bullets, desperate:
— Chef, table twelve wants you to write "I love you, Kimberley" in raspberry coulis on the plate.
What am I now, a fucking calligrapher?

Meanwhile, I'm losing my voice screaming:
— Fire the beef!
— Who stole my goddamn beets?
— Why is this dessert frozen like a brick?
The brigade's circling the drain, on the edge of a collective breakdown.
The dishwasher is threatening to quit.
The sous-chef is avoiding me like I've got rabies.
It's not a kitchen anymore—it's an asylum.
A fucking madhouse.

Meanwhile, in the dining room, it's pure theater.
Some couples lean into it, playing their roles perfectly.
You've got the love-struck ones picking petals.
Others pretending to love each other or silently hating each other.
Some are faking passion, and some are divorcing in silence;
Others are scrolling their phones while the plates I just sent are getting cold. And I'm foaming with rage as they snap pics of my food instead of eating it.
I swear, I have stopped counting the times I've fantasized about hurling an iPhone into the deep fryer.
Usually there is always a moment when I pray that they don't start fighting between the starter and the main.
Or worse, one dumps the other during dessert.
Because it happens, I am dead.

Not because the food was bad. But because their relationship is in the gutter, and ultimately, I'll be the one responsible if there is a review.
Finally, at midnight, the last lava cake leaves the pass.
Think it's over? Nope.
Now here come the complaints.
— The steak was overcooked.
— Dessert is too sweet.
— The ambiance is not romantic enough.

By the end you're wrecked. You are reeking of truffle oil, your arms are burned, your feet are crushed, and your brain is flashing in red.
Everyone got slammed so an eighty-dollar dinner could save or sink a relationship that was already tanked.
For real, I've had customers tell me they broke up because of Valentine's dinner.

And guess what?
Tomorrow it's brunch, so if you think you'll catch a break, keep on dreaming, buddy.
No break. No mercy. Just more pain.
So come on then.
Bring your broken hearts.
Bring your idiotic requests.
Bring your garlic-free, onion-free, and fun-free demands.
The chef's waiting.
I'll be here.
Knives sharpened.

Music of the blades

As far back as I can remember, basically since I grew a few hairs on my chin, I've been possessed by three things:
Food. Music. Chaos.
A burning, instinctive trio.
Those are my drugs.
I need my fix every day.
And yesterday, something hit me out of nowhere.
Not a candlelit revelation but a filthy one. It was not clean, not pure, not holy. There were no angels, no halos. More like an epiphany that smelled like duck fat.
Just a greasy slap between three cuts, two sauces, and a pot of veal stock that reeked of marrow.
Sticky, gooey, and savory.

Let me set the scene.
The kitchen.
It's pre-service prep on Saturday night.
That weird suspended moment between tension and silence, like a dead zone. A lull, where chaos and harmony are screwing with each other.
The kitchen is still purring, knives are clacking gently on the cutting boards, fridges are humming, and stale coffees are staring right back at you.
We're counting proteins, checking sauces, slicing, trimming, and prepping.
Getting ready. Warming up. It's rehearsal time, baby.

Then as always around that time, I put my phone on the pass. I connect it to the speakers. And I press play and crank the kitchen playlist at full blast.
A sacred, pure mix of hits and rock 'n' roll so filthy, it should probably be banned by the Geneva Convention. So loud and powerful that the four busted speakers shake the grease from the ceiling and rattle the walls.

Here's how it works.
Rule number one:
The chef—me. The Springsteen in a white apron, worn blades, and a black jacket decides how many tracks we need.
Then we divide that number by the amount of soldiers on the line, and each of them throws in their poison. Usually depending on our mood and the prep mountain in front of us.
Listen, you don't choose ZZ Top for filleting a fish, and you don't break down a primal cut into ribeyes with Barry White.
So we dump it all in, we mix, we press play, and we suffer the consequences.
That's when you discover the truth.
When you find out the guy next to you, who is your savior in the weeds, the one who keeps your ass alive on the line, actually listens to Michael Bolton or Kenny G... by choice.
It's hilarious, revealing, and traumatic.
You don't look at him quite the same afterward.
It's like catching your father in lingerie or watching your dog lick an electrical socket.

It scars you.
You take a step back, maybe shed a tear, and you laugh your ass off.
But we don't mock, and you don't say a word.
That's rule number two.

Because music in a kitchen is more than background noise. For us, it's team cement; it's glue for the gang. It feeds the soul and the ears.
And food...well, food is music you chew.
Don't we talk about the musicality of a dish, about balance, and about rhythm?
You see, I'm not just talking shit.
Every dish is a melody, and every sauce is a riff.
Cooking is harmony or cacophony—nothing in between.

So we cobble together a sonic hell on the fly, made of the blazing genius of the seventies, the lightning strikes of the eighties, and the raw punch of the nineties.
The Stones. Bowie. Led Zeppelin. Hendrix. James Brown. U2. AC/DC. And of course, the chef's touch—the absolute crown jewel: Prince.
Oldies but goodies.
Songs that punch and smash—because we know tonight there's going to be blood and smoke. It's going to be brutal.
The reservations are through the roof, deliveries came late, and we've got a shitload to do in no time at all.

Between prep tasks, we sing, we yell, and we howl like calves heading to slaughter. We butcher every track with heart, joy, and good spirit.
It's pure sabotage.
Some of us even dance. Well, if you can call that thing "dancing." It looked like a drunk flamingo trying to fuck a blender.
Even Mick Jagger would probably walk out, confused and slightly disturbed, witnessing an epileptic giraffe humping an espresso machine.
And right then, as I am looking at my band of lunatics in the chaos, it hits me like a knife in the ribs:
We're not just a brigade; we're more than a crew.
We are a loud, messy, beer-soaked rock'n'roll band.

When the musical carnage dies down, we step out for a break. A cigarette in one hand and liquid poison in the other, we talk about music. The real stuff: the legends, dinosaurs, and gods of feedback, fueled by whisky and reverb.
Someone throws out:
— Can you imagine? Their lives, albums, the tours...
I stand up like some half-cooked prophet, dish towel over my shoulder like a guitar strap, and I shout:
—No need to imagine. That's our fucking life.
Half are laughing hysterically; the other stands there, looking at me, baffled.
I play guitar, so they think I'm joking.

But I stare them dead in the eye, and I double down.
— All of us, man. We're rock stars. You just forgot.
Blank stares. The awkward pause is turning into an embarrassing silence. So I push further, and I go full preacher mode.
The menu? That's the album.
Each dish is a track.
Lyrics and music: protein and garnish.
Recording and production: plating and all the decorative bullshit.
The tour? Service after service, seven nights a week. Raw, no encore.
And the weekend's special; that's the surprise single.
Sometimes, it's a hit, a plate that kills, or a solo that sticks in the client's head all night.
Other times, a flop. A complete fuck-up etched into our memory, wrecking the morale for the evening.
And we throw it and play it live, no matter what.
The rest? Just noise.
And I wrap up my little rant by saying:
—All of us chefs de partie, pastry chefs, dishwashers, sous-chefs, and head chefs—we are the Foo Fighters of food.
Standing tall, knives ready, still sending plates like power chords.
No groupies; just scars and a waitress giving you the side-eye because you reek like fryer oil.
No Grammys, no trophies; just cuts, burns,
And aprons on, ready to fire the next service.

And like any gang, we love each other. But sometimes we fight, and we make up with shots.

We keep debating and joking about who's who, what band we'd be in, which artist, and which instrument we'd pick. We're laughing our asses off as we head back inside. We go back to our duties, and I take a look at the clock.
Shit, service starts in an hour—we have to pick up the pace; it's time to haul ass.
So, we work like a band:
—The drummer?
The sous-chef keeps it tight and makes it snap. It's got to be steady, or we're dead.
—The bassist?
The dishwasher—without him, nothing holds. Unseen but keeping the whole fucking mess together.
—The lead guitarist?
The pastry chef was always the weird one in his corner, offbeat, in his own sugary world.
—The frontman?
The head chef—me. I yell, I conduct, and I drive the show, and if the dining room screams too loud, I crank it higher. Some nights I'm Jagger, shaking my ass and screaming at the crowd. Other nights, Angus Young is manic and unhinged.
But lately? I feel more like Bono, because we're short-handed, and there are four of us doing the work of six. But we still have to pretend to be in a stadium when we're really four guys playing in a garage.

Because a service is like a rock concert.

It's live. No playback, no redo. You hit the stage, the crowd's there, and you've only got two hours to throw down and burn it all.

Most of the time it's a well-oiled machine. A sound-and-light show tuned down to the millimeter. But sometimes it turns into total improvisation—messy, chaotic, and sweaty.

But you give it all—energy, talent, soul, sweat, voice, and guts. And by the end, you're drenched, drained, and wiped out.

You didn't just cook—you performed.

That's why I can't stand silent kitchens.

A kitchen without music is like a song without a guitar or a dish without sauce. It's flat. Depressing.

No music? No pulse.

Real ones know: drop some Led Zep in the heat of the shift, and it's a defibrillator; it's CPR.

Throw on a David Gilmour solo—it's like morphine, and you survive anything, even vegans allergic to flavor or lactose-intolerant snowflakes whining about pepper.

Some meditate to recenter. Me? Pink Floyd aligns my chakras.

Hendrix calms me down.

Prince makes me want to torch it all, but with style.

Cooking is like rock 'n' roll. It's messy. Loud. Violent. Beautiful.

It's cocaine for the soul;

It's gasoline for the brain.

It's alive.
It's highs and crashes.
It's stage-diving into the chaos of a raging crowd.

Shit. I am talking and talking, and I just lost track of time. I've got to go. Service is about to start. My crew is ready, and I can feel the tension is rising. And I don't want to miss our special moment before the curtain goes up.
It's always the same routine:

Like the Stones suiting up, we adjust our jackets.
Jagger grabs the mic;
Richards clutches his Telecaster like his life depends on it.
We grab our knives, sharpen them, and wipe the blades one last time before stepping into the arena.
We hear the fans are coming in; they are sitting down, and they are ordering drinks while they wait for the big guns to drop the hits.
Suddenly the printer rattles off a couple of tickets; it sounds like the crowd's roaring hot.
We are ready.
We line up for our Saturday-night ritual.
Rags at the hip, knives raised like guitars, hearts pumping hard and brains set to blow.
We crank the speakers and they spit the same song we always blast before the Saturday night service.
We clap each other on the back, looking each other in the eye like warriors juiced on anxiety and adrenaline.

And like AC/DC, right before the cannons explode and Angus Young goes ballistic, we, gladiators of the béchamel, roar our steroidal tribal chant.
The title of our greasy anthem that reeks of grease, fire, and brotherhood
The only gospel that matters in the kitchen at that minute:
We yell in unison:
— ♫ *For Those About to Rock (We Salute You).*

U.S.A.
United States Of Allergies

! WARNING !

"The second I started this chapter, I realized this wasn't going to be a delicate operation—this is heavy-duty demolition. Given the sheer scale of the damage and the mountain of rubble I have to move, I knew right away a standard shovel wouldn't cut it. So, I went and got the Extra-Large model.
Before I start, get the mop ready. You're going to need a lot of bleach to clean up after me.

Welcome to the U.S.A. in twenty twenty-five, where cooking in a restaurant isn't an art anymore—it's litigation.
Because every plate is a booby trap.
Every entrée is a potential lawsuit.
We've traded flavor for fear, taste for trauma.
We went from pleasure to panic.
"Bon appétit" has been replaced by "Warning, possible danger."

In France, at least, it's simple.
On the ticket you receive, there's a starter, a main course, a cooking temperature, and a dessert.
Once in a while a real allergy is mentioned, you raise an eyebrow, say "OK," and that's it. Then you go back to cooking like good soldiers.

Here, nowadays, an order ticket looks like a culinary prescription, at best. A medical thesis, at worst.
As for the menu, it's no longer a promise of pleasure—it's a triage sheet. A digestive compatibility grid with footnotes longer than the Bible.
It's the Declaration of Human Rights, foodie edition.
A diplomatic treaty of feelings and well-being written in Arial eight with more asterisks than a cell phone contract.

 Gluten-free

 Vegan

Animal products

Vegetarian

May contain traces of independent thought

And this nightmare starts in the dining room with the servers, poor souls in black aprons.
Don't even think about starting service with half a pen and a used notepad.
No.
It's one pen per table and a fresh pad for two covers, or they're dead.
They take orders with fear in their eyes, writing until their hands cramp, rereading, and repeating, terrified of messing up.
Then they run to the bathroom, grab their phone, and confirm a therapy appointment for their PTSD.

Honestly, I feel for them.
And when they come back into the kitchen:
— Chef, excuse me... Is there milk in butter?
— Yeah, genius. It's not made from apples.

For us cooks, same shit, different toilet.
With all the modifications and the "Could you just?" if you don't start service with four rolls of thermal paper, you're screwed six ways from Sunday. You won't last two hours.
And when the printer starts spitting tickets like a machine gun, each dumber than the last, I've got two options:
Either I slit my wrists with my chef knife,
Or I calmly ask the waiter if the customer came here to eat, to detox, or to attend a wellness retreat.

Now listen, I'm not talking about real allergies:
Shellfish, nuts, lactose intolerance, and celiac disease.
People who blow up like a balloon if a shrimp touches their plate.
That's real. We adapt, we protect, we take care of you. Anaphylactic shock is serious.
Let me repeat for the digital snipers so I don't get crucified on social media:
Some allergies are serious, and you don't fuck around with that.
But the others... the rest. Those for whom it's no longer a medical emergency or an anaphylactic crisis, but an identity crisis.

It's funny, though, how these "intolerant" people aren't always intolerant to pleasure.
I've seen some "gluten-free" people are knocking back pints of draft beer.
Some "lactose intolerant" guests finish dinner with a scoop of ice cream and ask for whipped cream.

I swear to God it turns into a circus.
I've cooked egg-white omelets that made me want to dive headfirst into the fryer.
Gluten-free pancakes that tasted like Styrofoam coasters.
I've tasted almond-milk cappuccinos with soy foam—basically lukewarm piss in a cup.
All because Table Eleven thinks they have a "sensitivity."

That brings us to the glutenophobes.
Gluten has become Voldemort—he-who-must-not-be-named.
Half of them don't even know what gluten is.
Ask them, and they freeze like a rabbit in headlights.
According to them, they're all intolerant.
Bullshit. You're just a pain in the ass.
Many people avoid gluten without any medical diagnosis. There are more people claiming gluten sensitivity than people actually sick.
As a result, gluten-free has become a gigantic market because they managed to turn their allergies into a trend.
We're approaching the pure essence of absurdity.

It has become a status symbol.
It's fashionable.
A lifestyle.
Sensitivity is the new Rolex.
Only one percent of the world's population is actually allergic to gluten. And tonight they're all in my restaurant?
Did they come here by bus or what?

And then we have the veganarchists.
My favorites, they make my head spin.
The kings of carnage.
The queens of culinary tantrums.
The evangelists who roll into the restaurant at nine p.m. on a Saturday, right in the middle of hell. And generally speaking, they don't give a damn about your menu. They'll take it out of politeness, but they're going to order their own.
If you open a restaurant nowadays, you don't need a team anymore; you need an invasion army.
One chef per table, one server per guest.
And it goes like this:
—Can you ask the chef if he could make us a vegan dish but not too aggressive in the cooking? And nothing processed, only local ingredients, ethical, gender-neutral, and low-carbon footprint.
Once again, I'm not making this up.

Dear Customers,
This is a restaurant, not a Tibetan spa. I'm neither a druid nor a shaman. So cut the crap.
Especially since these Sunday vegans hit the McDonald's drive-thru on weekdays for a square

egg sandwich drowned in ketchup, washed down with a fourteen-syllable iced coffee.
But on Sunday at lunch, they want you to redo their risotto because chicken stock...well...is animal suffering, isn't it?
These people are smoothie missionaries.
For them, quinoa is a spiritual sacrament.

An example? Of course.
And I insist that every bit of the following has actually happened. I've heard it and seen it.
A vegan warrior has just sat down at a table with her burlap tote bag and an inquisitorial stare that starts judging you the second you say, "Hello."
With a passive-aggressive wattage stronger than Turkish coffee, she scans the menu as if she were looking for war crimes.
And then you get a surreal conversation:
— Is the tofu fermented?
— Local?
— Free of symbolic violence?
— Was the salad washed with decarbonated water?
— Is the dishware cleaned with products tested on animals?
The server just stares at her, dumbfounded, and then comes back to repeat all this to me in the kitchen because he has no idea what he can even suggest to her.
Me?
My fuse is blown, and I start thinking that one day we might have to cook without gas and rub two

rocks together to start a fire... just to make them happy.
Shit. I'd rather drown in melted butter than live in lukewarm tofu.

And the salad of the day? Forget it.
You're scared to add a hard-boiled egg like it's a live grenade. You'd have to print a fucking pivot table just to explain what's in it.
— Chef, the lady wants to know if the salad contains celery.
— No. There isn't any.
— And if it came into contact with celery?
— Well... it's friends with a stalk. Don't worry, it's platonic.
Another true story.

But the grand prize always goes to one special category that seems to have escaped from an asylum:
The guests who want "without" and "with."
Flexitarians, meaning they do whatever the fuck they want whenever the fuck it suits them.
Usually without a shred of sense of humor as well.
— Table twenty-four wants a steak well-done.
But...
Without salt.
Without garlic.
Without sauce.
Without fat.
Grilled, but not too much, because the guest suffers from social hyperthermia.

No vinegar in the sauce or the dressing—childhood trauma.
Bread without yeast, without wheat... and without water—he's hydrophobic.
Make sure the sides are not too hot either—he's afraid of steam.
And please keep the dining room quiet. He's allergic to noise, order, and human contact.
Get a fucking grip.
And they explain all this calmly, like they're defusing a bomb.
This isn't an order anymore; it's a hostage negotiation.
But when the plate arrives?
They ask for grated cheese, mustard, and ketchup.
At that point your brain does a triple backflip, and you stare at your brigade, wondering if you're on "Pranked."
No. It's real. And it's every day.

And on top of that, you have to endure the cults and their laundry list:
Throw in keto, paleo, low-carb, plant-based, dairy-free, soy-free, GMO-free, pesticide-free, hormone-free, and flavor-free.
Basically, a buffet of hysteria where the only thing guaranteed is... misery.
Well, you know what?
I've become a victim too.
Like you, I now have my own allergy.
To bullshit.
Chronic and irreversible.

But most of all, I've become intolerant to their sensitivities.

Every ticket I read makes me think of the Bowie song: ♫ *I'm Afraid of Americans.*
When I listen to it, paranoia crawls over me like an invisible army.
Bowie doesn't scream—he whispers, with a pale and robotic voice. He smothers you with a dull thump, an era that's absurd, uniform, and under constant surveillance, junked on permanent control.
He says what no one dares to say out loud: that we live in a world that's policed, freaked out, and ridiculous.
It's my panic attack in stereo, because now, I freak out too. I am afraid.
Not of Americans, but of what we've done to food.
A hygienic, sanitized, paranoid nightmare, pasteurized and sponsored by intolerance.
Every plate is suspect.
Every ingredient is a threat.
Every customer has a data sensor linked to an app tracking their anxiety in real time
And that title fits this chapter perfectly. Like a latex glove, skin-tight and impossible to rip off, even with your teeth.

The conclusion is simple
The worst intolerance of all is hypocrisy.
We live in a time where everyone wants to eat differently, but nobody wants to admit that eating is visceral.

It’s salty. It’s spicy. It’s sweet.
It’s raw or cooked.
It’s alive or dead.
They want emotions without fat.
Memories without sugar.
Plates that don't challenge them—just politely respect them and don't disturb anything.
The truth is, great dishes are like great chefs—they grab you, or they bore you, but they leave a mark.
Today you don’t write a menu anymore; you draft a goddamn charter of dietary tolerance like a fragile diplomatic balance.
You apologize for cooking. You adjust, disinfect, and correct, and you spend more time reading restrictions than plating dishes.
And the worst part?
Nobody actually enjoys their food anymore.

But I didn’t sign up for that.
I didn’t sign up to manage dietary anxiety.
I signed up to send out plates that make memories bleed.
To put a tear in the eye of a guy who hasn’t cried in twenty years.
To hurl someone straight back to the Sunday kitchen of their childhood without even understanding why.
So yeah, I’ll keep cooking with butter and cream.
With love and a little bit of rage.
I will keep serving dishes that stick to your teeth and your heart.

Because I love you. And I do this for your own good.
So take risks; you will see... Flavor and sauce are good for the soul.
You have to understand that a kitchen isn't an emotional detox center. It's not the United Nations, and it sure as hell isn't a confessional. We're here for pleasure, not for soul purification or cleansing your aura.
And if you've got more demands than NASA's technical specs, maybe you're in the wrong place. Maybe it just isn't your spot.
US, we are definitely not here to get a Facebook pat on the head but to see joy and pleasure on faces.
And don't look at me with pity, like I'm some medieval torturer just because I dared to cook a ribeye.

I have a little confession straight from the heart. There's a little rhyme for all my American patients that I've always dreamed of printing on the menu in red, bold letters, size seventy-two.

If you're afraid to eat, that's fine.
My kitchen isn't your safety line.
Stay home, cook your vegan treats,
Or go online and order Uber Eats.
But If you show up in my restaurant by chance,
Know I don't do therapy, and I don't cook plants.

Back to work.

Star Wars

Internet strikes back

! WARNING !

Well, I still have my shovel in hand from the previous chapter; might as well excavate a bit deeper and see what we can dig out.

I have to say everything you're about to read is true—seen, heard, and happened; otherwise, it's not fun.

Fun, well... for some of us who've lived it and remember it.

Less fun for the others who'll recognize themselves.

Sorry in advance—it's going to sting a little.

You've asked for it.

Back in the day, regarding food critics, it was simple. We had The Michelin Guide, Zagat, The New York Times, New York Magazine, Food & Wine, The New Yorker, the L.A. Times, and Gourmet Mag.

They knew what they were talking about; they were not amateurs. They were pros, tough guys, biters, and sharp. And sometimes assassins. Godfathers, old-school hitmen of gastronomy. You were judged on the plate, the taste, the presentation, and the service. The smile of the tablecloth and the hostess's polish.

Or the other way around.

It was a square system, and at least it was a fair game. The verdict boiled down to one thing: swim or sink.
Every year, restaurant owners and chefs were sweating bullets waiting for the stars to show up.
A good review?
Full house for months.
A bad one?
Funeral flowers, a shovel of dirt, and a first-class burial, and the chef's next stop would be the closest unemployment office.
Thank you, goodbye, and don't call us back.
It was our ratings show—like film reviews.
Flop, masterpiece, decent time, or "go if the lights are on." And sometimes worse: "massive turd, don't even think about it."

Today?
The rules are gone.
It's open carry, shoot-on-sight in every direction at once. No quarter, no mercy. No survivors.
"Women and children first" is a line from ancient history.
The reason?
Two hundred million Americans follow football.
That's two hundred million coaches.
Restaurants? Same thing.
Two hundred million customers—two hundred million critics.
What does that mean?
It means that after one mouthful, some clueless penguin with no palate and no diploma can

destroy your restaurant on a star-rating app and an iPhone.
Sometimes they don't need balls or courage either. Just a keyboard, a username, and a grudge as a payback.
No hello, no thank you—just bye-bye.

And 🎵 *Acrobat* by U2 is the anthem of this crooked era. It's not a hit, not an easy track, but it's a masterpiece.
Bono sings of disillusion, truth collapsing, and invisible judges watching and ruling without understanding.
That's exactly the soundtrack we need: the sound of a fall into the digital void.
And you, the chef, you're out there, tightrope-walking on barbed wire, trying to survive the avalanche of pixels, venom emojis, and passive-aggressive smileys.
Welcome to the virtual jungle—where you don't die of a snakebite.
You die of a one-star review.

And TripAdvisor, Yelp, Google, Uber Eats, Instagram, and TikTok are the battleships of this army of executioners without remorse.
Add your mom, your cousin, and the cat—everyone's got a hot take to post.
Meanwhile, you're juggling tickets and filling orders and dealing with meltdowns when a couple strolls in on a Saturday night.
It's their one date night of the week.
So, it's party time:

Him: hip, trimmed lumberjack beard, tight suit squeezed into ankle-flasher pants and tassel loafers, no socks.
He's been chewing rice cakes to fit into his kid brother's shirt and keep his breath from killing the mood. So yeah, he's on edge, restless, and circling—starving with an empty stomach.

Yeah, I know—I've got a thing with beards.
A guy hiding behind a shrub—unless he's Gandalf or Chewbacca—makes me suspicious.

Her—she needed an hour and thirty minutes to get ready. Didn't eat all day to slip into the dress, and she's fresh from the hair salon.
But it's raining, and there's no valet.
So, the car fight is on because now they're circling for the closest spot to the restaurant to save the blowout from death row.
Tension is building.
But by the time they hit the door, it's DEFCON TWO.

They sit at the "view" window table he booked to impress her, you know, for the wow effect.
Two minutes later, he's whining there's a draft down there...by his ankles.
Of course, there's a draft—it's April, and you're not wearing socks. Dumbass.
They're moved to the heated patio, with a killer view—perfect, right?

Except Mr. Zen Energy, whose frequency is synced to the latest feng shui podcast, now complains about people smoking—the cigarette smell ruins his inner mantra.
After six table changes in eight minutes, the hostess lost her sense of humor, and her smile is long gone, obviously.
And voilà—you've got your first review of the evening:
"Staff is helpful but not very friendly."
The disaster kicks off. War is on.

They crack jokes and smile at the table, but inside they're boiling, because everything must be tip-top.
The food better be to their taste.
The service needs to be fast but at their pace.
And the server must be funny but not funnier than him.
Cocktails are required to look like the ones they had on vacation.
Wine at their preferred temp, and the music in the background is just lounge-y enough—but not too much.
Otherwise you'll wake up to a gift to read.
a short, cryptic, venomous comment.

Because today every guest is a sniper.
A wrinkle in the cloth: Wham.
The sauce is a bit salty; BAM.
The server didn't laugh at his joke. Thank you, ma'am.

Mint in the mojito? Two stars—offensive to my Aries sun and Capricorn ascendant.
Right in your face.
You can grind fourteen hours straight, have busted your ass, haven't pissed since noon, and tank three rushes and ten endless monster tickets, then sit in the kitchen and read the following:
– Food was good, but the ambiance was too loud; I couldn't hear myself think.
– The cook seemed stressed (I didn't see him, but I could tell).
– No chili-free vegan option for my dog; I am disappointed. I talked to the chef about it; he did not look very interested.

And sometimes you even did do anything wrong.
The dude brings a date, tries to impress her, plays the big shot, and tells her to order anything she likes.
She goes for caviar, lobster, desserts, and top-shelf bubbles.
He has a hot flash when the bill lands and smacks his orbit.
Review before he faints.
– Crazy expensive for what it is, way overpriced. Two stars.
You cooked like a god, but your rating takes the bullet.
What do you want to do? You take the hit and move on.
And if a review says the dish was over-seasoned?
The next day, your manager comes in:
– We need to cut the salt. It looks bad now.

Huh? What?
I swear to God, it's all true.
I know some chefs who are now cooking without pepper just to avoid more complications.

To be fair, sometimes we mess up.
The server forgot to fire a table, and the couple are about to open their jugulars with a coffee spoon. They're starving; they've been waiting for their meals for twenty-six minutes with nothing in front of them but thin air and an empty basket of bread.
You sent the dish... drenched in sauce when he wanted the sauce on the side.
That's the game. Everybody drops the ball.
It happens.
And yes—Sure, there are legit cases—
The menu is boring
The service is a total disaster.
The food tastes bland or like shit depending on what you order.
They exist.
It happens actually more than you think

I think that most reviews aren't judging food—they're judging a moment, an ego.
Sometimes it's just people needing attention.
A soda does not have enough ice.
Hot dish served... too hot.
Lighting that's too honest and doesn't hide a cold sore.
Brace yourself—shit's going to splatter online.

Nowadays, these stars aren't medals anymore—they're missiles. But forget about surgical strikes; it's more like weapons of mass culinary destruction.
So in kitchens, now we feel like we are in Star Wars. The Death Star isn't a planet—it's an app. That planet-killer beam is a one-star dump posted from a bathroom stall.
And if you feel like answering the review with an email—forget it; you need a lightsaber.

Sometimes I wonder if I'm a dying species.
When I eat somewhere, I like it or I don't. That's it. I don't go online to write a novel about my digestion.
I never understood this obsession to review and to share everything now, to narrate your life and your plate on social media.
It's insane.
As if the world would collapse if Kevin, twenty-four years old and a marketing assistant intern, didn't conduct a full metaphysical thesis on his tomato mozzarella.
Spoiler alert: nobody gives a fuck, kiddo.
It reminds me of the reason why I like wildlife documentaries; herd behavior fascinates me.
And we humans are no exception.
One good review and boom—everyone follows, even if the food is awful.
— Great lighting, and the music had a nice vibe. My dish? Uh... I don't really remember. Actually, I wasn't very hungry. But the atmosphere was cool. So... four stars.

The next day, it's fully booked.
Kill me, kill me now, I beg you.

And to finish the carnage, here comes a new breed of brainless idiots, the final mutation, as I like to call them.
Our new "friends," the foodies.
The pic addicts. The Instagram children.
The influencers of intergalactic bullshit—part-time leeches angling for a free meal.
A cross between a tweet addict, a pic maniac, and a smug clown on Xanax who thinks he's a food critic.
They sit down, phone ready, flash on, frame set, and angles perfect. They photograph everything—the salt shaker, the pepper mill, the cutlery. Even the goddamn glass of water.
Before they even taste anything, they judge the sauce color, the coriander placement, and the plate symmetry.
They chew with their followers.
They taste their stories.
Digests with their posts,
They judge with filters.
And shit with a hashtag.
They analyze food like Fellini stuck in a food court.
The Scorsese of the feed.
The Coppola of the post.
The Tarantino of the interstellar void.
Meanwhile, you've sweated blood and butter to build a solid, honest plate...but he (or she) doesn't give a damn.

What matters? That it "looks good on screen."

— Chef, don't you think the plate looks a little sad?
— No, it's not sad, and it's not depressed either. And by the way, it's not a plate. It's a braised short rib. So, eat it and leave it the fuck alone.
And my favorite part, when the check lands:
— I'll give you a great post, a glowing review, on my blog. I will bring you traffic.
Translation: You pick up the bill, big guy, or else.
And when you ask, "Was it good?"
— Dunno, I didn't touch it. I'm not here to eat; I'm here to influence.
When we get these kinds of superstars, we want to do the same thing they do.
Take a picture of them before having the pleasure of tasting their conversation.

Despite all this crap, I still believe most restaurant folks—kitchen or floor—try their best.
Aside from a few cave trolls who don't give a damn. But if you hate this job, if it's just to pay bills, the grind breaks you out mid-flight. You don't last.
Look, not all customers are like this. Even with their little quirks.
Know we're here to make you happy. To give you a good time. But a restaurant is alive, so yeah, sometimes we screw up.
Other times we send a plate that could've saved your day, and you scroll for twenty minutes, then toss it back and tell the waiter:

— It's cold.
We wanted stars for our plates, not stars crashing into our faces like digital time bombs.
Today, one frustrated guest equals one click, and it's Hiroshima in the kitchen.

Whatever.
We keep going. We cook. We send it.
Because despite everything... The Force is still with us.
So, Darth Vader—
If you don't like it, say so. And we'll do better next time.
If you do like it, then look your server in the eye, smile, and slide them a quiet
— That was great. My compliments to the chef.
With luck, chances are that you might get a coffee or a little drink on the house from a Jedi.
And you'll go home happy
So do we.
Because we saved the galaxy.

Back then,

When it was better burnt

! WARNING !

Heads up, in this chapter there's a lot of fat to chew and plenty of shovel blows coming your way. So if you need to piss, smoke a cigarette, pour yourself another drink, or grab a bag of chips... now's the time.

Let's step out of the kitchen for a minute—come on, let's grab a drink at the bar. We'll cool off and talk a bit, because I've got a confession to make.
This era wears me out.
It exhausts me. It drains me.
You can't say shit anymore. Everything's sanitized, deodorized, and tasteless.
And it drives me mad.
We're careful about everything, all the time. We walk on eggshells twenty-four / seven, and we tiptoe around everything all the time. We pick our words like we plate a dish for social media.
And if you want to be sure not to offend anyone today, stop talking and learn sign language. And even then... watch your middle finger.
Everything has to be explained; it needs a disclaimer.
Every word is a possible explosion, a landmine.
Every joke is a potential complaint or a police report waiting to happen.
You raise your voice, you're toxic, and they send you to a "non-violent seminar."

You yell "pick up" at the pass in the kitchen, and everyone stares at you like you just threw a baby in the fryer.
You smoke a cigarette on your break, and some well-meaning manager hands you a printed lecture about the dangers of tobacco.

We live apologizing. We cook, asking for forgiveness. We have to be inclusive and inspiring.
Everything is calibrated, marketed, pasteurized, and polished.
And the chefs have been turned into "low-pressure" brand ambassadors. Gentle little coaches smiling like an organic slogan for cereals. Wearing freshly ironed jackets and sneakers whiter than a yoga studio. They are working in kitchens cleaner than operating rooms—without noise, smell, rage, or balls.
They design menus with low carbon footprints. Plates, perfectly framed for photos, where most of the effort is focused on how they look, not on how they taste.
It has become more profitable to have a great photographer and a half-assed chef than the other way around.
To tell you the truth, I am not sure where all this is going, but it's quite a shock. Because it's very different from the world I used to live in.

I was born in the seventies and nurtured in the eighties.

But I lived the nineties and the first decade of two thousand full throttle.
I grew up in a world that smelled like cigarettes, lukewarm whiskey, blunt talk, and great music.
We'd fight at the fifteen-minute mark and laugh at the thirty-minute mark. Humor was a weapon —we laughed at everything, mostly ourselves.
You could drop a fucked-up joke and maybe eat a punch for it—but never a lawsuit.
It was filthy. Dirty.
But it was free.
Christ, I miss those years.

Dreams didn't cost much; rents were criminal but still doable.
Restaurants hadn't yet been invaded by influencers and kombucha sommeliers rebranding themselves as "fermentation consultants."
We didn't give a rat's ass about image.
There was no food styling, no dumb hashtags.
No storytelling.
And thank God, no Zoom meetings.
The restaurant industry was packed with borderline maniacs, live wires—wild lunatics.
Chefs or cooks who didn't bust their asses for "likes"—they worked to serve your food hot, good, and on time.
Services, where you risked a burn or brutal screaming, but boredom never made the menu.
A time when "chef" meant leader, not some LinkedIn ambassador of your brand or pitchman.

It wasn't a spa—it was a ring. You walked in to get hurt, to push yourself. Not to sit cross-legged, breathing love to cuddle your chakras.
Was it violent? Hell yeah.
Was it tough? Fuck yes.
But it forged beasts of cooks, not community managers in recyclable hats.

Do you want a sauce with your meal? Here try this one.
I'm warning you, it's not some lukewarm hollandaise at Sunday brunch but a fucking Molotov cocktail.
♫ *Rebel Yell* by Billy Idol—Now that's the soundtrack of kitchens and dining rooms reeking of adrenaline and revolt.
It's leather sticking to the skin and services spinning out at two hundred miles an hour with no brakes.
Billy howls like a rabid mutt; it slams like a brigade in full heat. It thumps like a chef smashing a fridge door open.
It's the anthem of the years we cooked and served with guts and insulted each other with respect.
When mistakes cost you a burn or a drop of blood, not a complaint form at HR.

Now don't misunderstand me; I am not bitter.
And yes, I am a little nostalgic. But mostly, I'm pissed.
Because they stole my job and replaced it with a bullshit marketing campaign.
Let me tell you something:

Whether in the kitchen or front of house, we weren't altar boys, but we made it no matter what.
We delivered. We gave it our all.
We ended the night drained, broken, wrecked sometimes, and wasted often—but proud and aligned with our values.
Why?
Because this craft is a drug.
And a curse.
A damn calling, like being a priest, a cop, or a teacher, and you need a thick skin to take it.
If you don't have it in your gut, go sell organic yogurt. It's not for everybody, and it's ok.
What bothers me a little is that I don't find that urgency anymore, that raw intensity in the restaurant's staff.

Except maybe in Gordon Ramsay.
In terms of untamed animals, he's worth watching.
A real talent and a big mouth.
He screams because nowadays everyone whispers.
He yells because he knows what it means to watch a service collapse, and he's given too much to let shit leave the pass.
Sure, he exaggerates and throws insults.
But he comes from the same world as me. One that teaches you to stand up and be proud of what you are, of who you are.
Because we know what it means to push out one hundred and fifty covers under fire without

whining. Without wellness coaches and Zen playlists. No Facebook sob stories in pastel words.
Ramsay? He throws the truth in your face.
It's brutal—yes.
But it's real.

And while we're at it, there's all the rest.
All these signs of our time that have been creeping in for years.
Yeah, I am switching gears, because this crap gets on my nerves. It's been stewing in me for a while.
Back in nineteen eighty-seven, we already had ♫ *Sign o' the Times.* Prince wasn't the funky preacher of ♫ *Let's Go Crazy* anymore. Four years after "Purple Rain," no more calls to burn it all down. To set the world on fire. Partying like it's ♫ *1999* is no longer on the agenda.
Now he's the chronicler of a disaster. Voice steady, scalpel in hand.
No pathos, no rage, just icy clarity.
A track like an autopsy report—dry tempo, minimal but with an impeccable groove, and notes as sharp as a chef's blade.
It's listing and dissecting the plagues; catastrophes roll by—AIDS, crack, and violence.
And that guitar in the background appears like a thin thread, a beacon of hope, that reminds us that once there was funk and once there was soul.

My signs of the times today?
The religion of ratings.
Back then we had consumer watchdogs.

Now? Millions of user reviews and opinions.
Influencers are firing shots of their plates like war reporters.
Amateur critics, convinced they have taste.
A bunch of idiots confusing opinion with knowledge.
Noise with truth.
The whole damn world has become a permanent jury, dropping three-word Google reviews and Uber Eats verdicts like quick-fire trials.
Hell, they even make you rate the delivery guy.
Didn't see him; food is at the door—but here, throw him some stars.
Why? Because he brought your order. So he deserves a medal for doing his job.
Another masterpiece on Uber—the snake eating its tail:
The driver and passenger rate each other.
Everybody's happy; everybody's got a star.
Fake equality achieved all around.
We've hit rock bottom.

And it's not just food.
It's everything: shops, hotels, candy bars, and dog food. I've even seen reviews for cat chow. How? Everyone feels obliged to spit their opinion, like it matters. People think their two cents are vital to society.
In French, we have a saying:
"Opinions are like assholes; everybody has one."
It has never been more true.

And what's this new stupidity I keep seeing in the streets?
People are strapping the dog leash around their waist like a jogging belt.
Hands-free authority on vacation and leadership on PTO.
Dog out front, they're just following, trailing behind.
Newsflash: the mutt isn't a Tesla!
Who's walking who, for fuck's sake? Huh?
If that's not collective resignation and complete surrender, I don't know what is.
Is it just me, or is everything going to shit?

But for me the cherry on top will remain this goddamn selfie craze. I am not even sure what to make of it anymore.
— Look at me, I exist; look at my amazing life.
And I thought I had an ego problem. Turns out, I'm a rookie compared to these clowns.
It says a lot about the world and the era we are living in.
Concerts aren't lived anymore; they're filmed. Thousands of arms up—not clapping, just holding phones. You pay a fortune to see your favorite artist and spend two hours capturing blurry shit you'll never rewatch.
But you'll post it—to prove you were there.
Museums? Same story.
Nobody looks at the paintings. We take a snap and move on. Like your phone's going to capture what your eyes didn't.

We don't live the moment—we store it for social validation.

I remember a time when, if you sat in front of a TV or a movie screen, it was to get entertained. Now we use it to stage ourselves and lay out our lives. We parade our daily load like mannequins in a shop window—as if we had something to sell. We want to be liked, to offer ourselves to the crowd. To please and to hawk it to passers-by to prove our existence isn't as vain and futile or meaningless as it feels.
We dress up and reinvent our lives because ours won't do. Because our real one isn't enough. Because truth doesn't cut it anymore.
We fill the void hoping someone, somewhere, will comment or drop a heart emoji.
We watch the world through a filter—either to protect ourselves or, worse, to convince ourselves we deserve a podium.
We've gone from
"I think, therefore I am."
to
"I've got a like, therefore I exist."
Welcome to modern philosophy. Descartes must be spinning in his grave.
If you don't know who Descartes is, google him; some reading won't do you any harm.

As for me, the only screen I care about now is total sunblock. To stop the rays of stupidity and the hollow vanity of this shallow-ass world. And I watch this culinary and digital circus from my

kitchen, hiding in plain sight. Sheltered from the void. In the shade of nothingness.
But I know there's no miracle coming, only a raw truth:
The fatality of a world changing for the worse.
And deep down, Prince had already warned us—if we don't pay attention, the signs of our times will mess with our minds.
If you listen to the song carefully, around the fourth minute and twenty seconds, the drums buck and sprint. It almost feels like it's not a musician behind it anymore. It sounds like nervous fingers hammering a plastic keyboard. Dropping final sentences from some couch.
Behind every hit is an opinion.
Behind every silence is the void behind the screen.
And that dry repetitive crack?
That's our swan song.

I'll be honest, I don't have patience for this shit anymore.
You really want to know what I miss?
The chaos.
The glorious mess of the good old days, when it was better, burned.
The golden age.
Not tweets, not wellness QR codes.
But phone booths and answering machines.
When you weren't there—you just weren't there.
And that was fine.
No—where are you?
No—why didn't you answer?
No—what are you doing?

Not your fucking problem, goddammit?
Today we have to be connected, available, and traceable.
Smartphone glued to our hand.
AirPods in our ears.
Connected ring, vibrating watch.
Dog on Wi-Fi, toothbrush on Bluetooth.
Even sperm doesn't get peace anymore. They're counted, tracked, and monitored.
You don't see people in the streets; you see zombies walking with eyes sucked into screens.
And when they lift their heads, it's to scream into their speakers. Like the whole world wants to hear about their lukewarm stories and mental loads.
Baby, we don't give a shit!
They make noise with their mouths, blowing air—like fans. It reminds me of a James Brown song:
♫ *Talkin' Loud and Sayin' Nothin'* ♫.

Wise words from Jean Gabin, a famous French actor:
— Speaking several languages is an asset, but knowing when to shut the fuck up is priceless.
I leave you all the time you need.
And since we're doing quotes, here's my favorite from Coluche, a French comedian:
—Amongst all those who have nothing to say, the smartest are the ones who stay silent.
It's simple math: talk nonsense all the time, and you'll say a lot of stupid things.
But noooooooo.
Let's tweet and retweet without taking the time to think.

But people don't take time anymore for anything.
They talk but they don't communicate.
And when you're at the restaurant, your wife's on Instagram, your kid's on his iPad, and you're in front of your plate.
Alone, like a schmuck.

Well, you know what?
This modern world, I don't like it.
This soft, mushy, and bland thing—I don't want it.
You can keep it.
It's boring, sterilized, slow, and pretentious. And it doesn't even taste like anything.
We're trying so hard to please everyone that we hide ourselves. No one catches fire.
And the worst?
Nobody laughs anymore. No lightness, no spirit, no second degree.
Everything feels like aggression.
Now an apprentice in the kitchen won't gut a chicken because it disturbs his "inner balance."
Don't ruffle him, or HR will ruffle you.
Back in my day, HR was the chef's office—and he sure as hell didn't sing you sweet words.
It was a full-blown dressing down; you got obliterated.

I am not saying the good old world was better.
But it was alive.
We lived and vibrated for a plate.
We cried with rage but not with shame.
We screamed, but we lived and breathed together.

I know I'm one of those who can't, won't, and will never pretend. That's why I could never build a culinary project. Because I could never smooth out my anger. I can't stand corporate bullshit.
I'm a guy with yesterday's world tattooed under his skin, staring at his era with quiet contempt.
And deep down... I became what I respected in others, a grumpy old bastard, a veteran.
The hell with it—that's why I'll always flare up.
I'll still ignite over a recipe—or a kid with grit and talent.
I still crack up at the same old dumb jokes.
And I'll still tell you to fuck off when you bust my balls or botch a station.
I am not complicated; I am not asking for much.
I just want us to close ranks and to stand together.
to love and to fight for the right reasons.
Service, taste, life, and the joy of being together.

I'm a chef, and I'll die a chef because I swore to burn in white or black. My jackets are black now.
Fuck it, color doesn't matter as long as I am burned alive.
I've seen kitchens that looked like looting scenes.
Chefs going down with their brigades.
Dishwashers, single-handedly saving services.
Brilliant kids slamming the door because some asshole broke them.
At fifty-three, with joints creaking and my liver bitching, I still got the rage.
I still get that chill at the moment of "fire!"
And as long as that chill's there, as long as I've got a knife, a hot stove, and a service to run, I'll stand

and fight until they put me out. Or until I got nothing left in the tank.
And when I fall, it won't be clean;
It'll be old-school.
With one last dish that reeks of life.
Head high.
Cigarette in one hand, and glass of wine in the other.
And a last burst of laughter.

I am done for this chapter.
This one's for all the rebels. The ones who cooked with rage, smashed plates, screamed, screwed up, came back, and are still standing in this fucked-up craft.
And for the others, the ones glued to their phones, plugged into their bullshit.
They can butter their quinoa.

Wait—scratch that.
Butter is happiness in a wrap.
It's banned now.

NEXT

Day off

Symptoms of an incurable psycho

Today, I'm not working.
So we're going to sit down, take it easy, have no stress, and spend a peaceful, quiet day.
It's my day off. Well... officially.
In reality, I'm on culinary quarantine.
My wife decided I had to rest. Do nothing.
I am strictly forbidden to touch a spatula, a whisk, an onion, or even a fucking toaster. She even hid the mandoline and slapped a padlock on the spice drawer.
Shit, now that I think of it, where the hell are my knives?

So here I am in the living room. I was allowed to sit on the designer couch that cost me an arm and a leg, which I'm usually strictly forbidden to.
It is suspicious. I'm wary.
I am staring at a dead TV, a cold espresso in my hands. I feel like a depressed monk, or worse... a customer.
My whole body itches—not the skin, the nerves.
My fingers and my muscles are begging for motion, smell, and action.
And I'm panicking at the thought the kids will eat chicken nuggets or a box of Mac and cheese.
I'm dreaming of a béarnaise, and I can smell it even though nothing's on the stove.
To tell you the truth, I think I'm losing it.

Rocky, my dog, stares at me, head tilted, and I see on his face that he's smirking. He knows.
He senses it; he knows the drill.
Shit's about to go sideways.

I get up and start roaming around the kitchen, pretending to look for a towel. I run my hand over the countertop like you'd stroke the hood of a fully loaded '66 Mustang. The one you've dreamed about your whole life and finally have in your garage.
The dog follows me.
I open the fridge. I am looking for something, but I don't know what.
I close it. I take a second to think.
I open it again and grab some leftover roast beef.
The dog looks at me, and I see it in his eyes. He's egging me on, pushing me.
—Go ahead, treat yourself!
Little Fucker.
The roast is studded with garlic.
I sniff the piece of meat like a junkie, and my eyes well up with tears, and I realize I'm drooling.
Damn.
I go to put it back in the fridge, and I mutter to myself:
– Come on, man, you can do this. You don't need to cook anything. No butter, no sauce. You're a free man.
To which my brain replies:
– We will see about that.
My daughter walks into the kitchen and stares at me.

— What are you doing, Dad?
Rocky turns his head away, faking innocence.
I jump and hide the chunk of meat behind my back.
— Nothing. I... I'm tidying up, organizing.
She squints, skeptical, and leaves with a bowl of chips.
I'm being watched; I can feel it. It's a trap.
My furry partner throws me a look of relief.
Close call; we just dodged disaster.

Noon hits, and I suggest cautiously
— So... I could make a quick risotto. Something simple, just a base... you know, just so...
My wife lifts her eyes from her book and gives me one look—one. Crystal clear.
Okay, I get it. I shut the fuck up.
And then, the ultimate punishment drops.
My wife decrees we're all going out to eat together.
— It'll do us good, and it'll relax you.
Crap!
I fall apart inside. It's like asking a surgeon to relax during his patient's autopsy.
But I nod in silence, because even if it's beyond me, I'm a professional. So I smile and play along.
I go back to plant my ass on that couch that wrecks my back. I stare at the immaculate white ceiling, waiting for the whole family to get ready to take off.

We arrive at the restaurant; the hostess greets us, and I sneak a glance behind her stand—it's spotless, tidy, and organized.
We head to our table.
Like a spy, I scan the room, but I don't check for emergency exits, no. I check the workstations, and as we walk towards our table, I scope the bar and sneak a peek at the pass.
We sit down.
The chairs aren't wobbly, there are no crumbs on the benches, and the floor is clean.
A quick glance into the kitchen: the chef looks calm... It won't last.
I know it.
We order—I go for beef tartare, my wife orders fish, and my daughter orders a burger and fries.
The restaurant fills up.
The server is rushing and starting to sweat.
I suffer for him; I want to help.
I see customers craning their heads—they need something.
He's overwhelmed, but where's the manager?
I read his movements like an old grimoire: he's on the edge.
I see everything. I feel everything. I'm in the dining room like a K-9 in a coke stash house. My eyelid twitches at every mistake; I log it all in my head.

The girls start whining:
— Where's the bottle of water?
It's been fifteen minutes.
And the wine? Still MIA.

The waiter is on the verge of a stroke. He brings plates and instantly takes them back—wrong table.
Ouch.
The kitchen starts buzzing, the chef waving his arms, the line cooks turning pale, and the sous-chef running.
Something's going to blow.
All I want is to grab an apron and ask the chef if I can jump on the line, the dish pit, the pantry, the garde manger, or anything; I don't care.
I'm like a junkie staring at his fix. I need my dose. I'm jonesing!

Plates land.
And the ride begins—the server forgets the bread and comes back without the wine.
He's sweating and over-smiling. He's out of breath and about to snap—I know a snow job when I see one.
And I, instead of eating, am spaced out. I am dissecting the plate, analyzing, and somatizing.
Then I clutch my napkin tight, grinding my teeth.
I feel the stress and the tension rising, but I stay locked and tuned to the kitchen.
Heads are spinning everywhere, a line cook throws his arms up, and a plate crashes. The chef yells something—I can't hear it, but I feel everything. Like I'm wired to their frequency, lip-reading the chaos.
The service is wobbling, the kitchen's rocking... but it holds.
I breathe with them, cheering them silently.

These guys, I know them. They'll drop dead before they let go. Not their style.
The chef's got his warrior face on.
And I realize that... a kitchen... It is beautiful from the outside too.

My dish is a touch too salty, but I don't care—I know the sweat behind it. I wolf down the meat and the mashed potatoes (made with butter) in three bites.
We order desserts to share. Coffee. Tea. The check.
I tell the waiter:
—Don't worry, kid, bring everything at once and take my card; it'll save you a trip.
I know there are customers waiting to be seated. Gotta turn those tables.
The waiter clears the table; I smile and slip in.
— Tell the chef it was great.
He walks off and chats at the pass for twenty seconds. The chef nods back and waves at me, out of breath.
We lock eyes.
I want to hug him, comfort him, give him courage, and thank him for service rendered to the brotherhood.

I get up and head to the bathroom, just to breathe, to cool down, or to escape the frenzy.
In the restroom, there's a piece of paper on the floor.
I pick it up—a reflex.
I tidy up the sink a bit—another reflex.

I look at myself in the mirror; I am red and sweating buckets.
I am talking to myself to calm down... but a towel answers.
Not good!
I blink.
I'm in a hallway.
No—in the kitchen.
Huh? My kitchen?
Is it the Saturday night service?
I don't know anymore.
I see the pass, a bell, and a ticket, and I reach out.
I plate, and I swirl a sauce. I send it, and I call for a pickup.
Rocky's there, wearing a toque, talking to me—he's tasted the mash. He says:
— More nutmeg, Chef.
I scream.
— Yes, Chef! at a trash can.
I pour a sauce into the sink.
I cook the meat with the blow dryer.
Fuck, that's it; I've lost it.

♫ *Comfortably Numb* slips into my skull like my dog into my bedroom to steal my socks. No noise, all feel: ninja style.
Holy hell, I have got Pink Floyd talking to me.
It soothes me. I feel like I've been shot up with a slow-release syringe of liquid indifference. A fix of pure madness, a dose of "I don't give a damn anymore."
I'm tightrope-walking over a minefield.

That song rocks me; it sounds like the soundtrack of the waiting room of hell for burned-out chefs. It's the score of a day off mutating into an existential nightmare.
I was supposed to recover, take my foot off the gas, and breathe. But my brain decided to rerun last night's service on loop.
My hands are plating invisible dishes, my back cracks at phantom calls, and my throat is screaming.
– "WHERE THE FUCK IS THE SOUS-CHEF?!"
Then David Gilmour lifts his guitar and drops a miracle in my ears. He delivers his solo like a prayer at the end of the service.
Floating. Inevitable. Perfect.
So I just stand there, stuck between two worlds.
Not really relaxed, not really aware.
I'm there, under the salamander, warm, slowly cooking.
Comfortably burnt.

I feel a hand on my shoulder.
My wife shakes me, and I snap back.
I'm in the living room, at home, sitting on the couch.
I'd dozed off.
She looks at me, worried.
– Are you okay? You are pale... You're sweating; we can order Uber Eats if you want?
I'm drenched; Rocky licks my hand.
I feel like I just crawled out of a nightmare in broad daylight.
I nod;

—Yeah. Let's order.
I am in for pizza!
My wife: —No, sushi!
My daughter: —Escargots and a ribeye with a peppercorn sauce.
Holy shit, there's still hope; not all is lost.
Everyone bickers; no one agrees, so war breaks out.
It's fucked. It's a mess.
My wife, fed up with the racket, tells me to do whatever I want.
I get up, and I try to hide a smile, but I can't. I head into the kitchen. I open the fridge, and Rocky plants himself next to me.
He knows that if he wants a little snack, it's better to stay close to the psycho.
So, I grab the pans, pull out a rack of lamb, and rub it with garlic.
The smell intoxicates me.
Potatoes, Provençal herbs... The butter sizzles in the pan.
The kitchen sings.
I turn on the hood.
She breathes.
It's alive again.
Chaos is back.
Hallelujah.

A four-legged miracle

Alright, this might be the shortest chapter in the book—and probably the dumbest.
But I don't care.
Because in this scorched-out insane world, there's more poetry in a dog than in everything and every so-called life coach will ever blabber online in this entire universe.
And to quote Bill Murray,
— I don't trust a person who doesn't like dogs, but I trust a dog who doesn't like a person.

Let me confess something.
For some chapters, I listened to a whole stack of songs among my favorites. The ones that hit the nerve, that made sense, that carried the same taste, the same punch.
Some of them marked me, made me dance or cry, or simply tagged along through years of my life.
I played them over and over, headphones tight, rewriting again and again until I hit the right tone. The right emotion.
But this one? This one jumped straight at my face.

At first, it started as a stupid idea.
I was dry and stuck on a chapter, and I needed a break to clear my head.
And like an idiot, in my infinite wisdom, I thought:

— Hell, I'll write about my dog; that'll crack me up.
He was lying at my feet, watching me with that lovesick gaze, saying without a word, "I'm here, buddy, don't worry. We're together. The rest doesn't matter."
Then I dug into my memory to look for songs about friendship and loyalty.
Then I thought of Dire Straits.

And as soon as I blasted ♫ *Brothers in Arms*. I started writing, glancing at him from time to time. Like I was pulling something out of him. And the more I watched him, the more what I was typing on my Mac started to make sense. It grew meat, depth, and soul.
Like a sauce that's reduced just right. Thick, glossy, and full of flavor.
The chapter poured out of me in half an hour.
Because that song—it's a slow dance for the walking wounded of the culinary war.
A song that lands when you've got no words left. When you're done yelling because your lungs are empty and you're done fighting because you're exhausted. But you still have just enough strength to love.
And in this collective hysteria, this self-obsessed world, if there's one living being who embodies that song better than anyone, it's a dog.
It's a loyal, furry companion who doesn't push you away when you stink, when you cry, or when you fail.

Rocky.

My Deluxe Golden Retriever.
Pure breed, pure bliss, pure grace. And one hundred percent pure love
Sent to Earth to save me one hair at a time.
He's beautiful like a Nordic god walking out of a spa.
He's got a canine supermodel face, hazel eyes brimming with tenderness, and walks like a king high on zen.

He cost me a kidney, half a liver—the good half—and my banker's soul. But I'd pay again, double, because Rocky isn't just my dog.
He's my four-legged miracle.
He's more loyal than anyone I've ever met.
Softer than a caress after a Saturday-night kitchen war.
More present than any shrink, quieter than a Tibetan monk, and stickier than my apron after a double shift.
Wherever I go, he's there. He follows me everywhere like a long-haired shadow. Always.
Not because he's annoying or needy, but because he loves me, brutally, unconditionally.
I take a piss—he guards the door.
I shower—he stands watch.
I take a dump—he stares with compassion. I'm embarrassed. He isn't.
Once, I sneezed. He whimpered—he thought I was dying.
He had tears in his eyes. So did I, a little.

He calms me. Me, the hothead, the borderline psycho. The guy who screams over a crooked plate.
He changes me because he grounds me; he reconnects me to the moment, to a breath, to something simple, pure, and real.
He doesn't judge me.
He doesn't send passive-aggressive messages and doesn't give a damn about social media.
All he wants is food, cuddles, and a peaceful life.
He's perfect, and his smile is worth every Michelin star on earth.
He sheds hair like I shed faith in humanity.
He looks at me like I'm a hero, even though I'm just a burned-out old war chef.
He protects me, and he's my spirit brother—wordless but overflowing with emotions.
He's my co-pilot of culinary explorations and my wingman of fridge leftovers. And he prefers a well-marbled ribeye over his overpriced food.
Just like me.

One day I caught him staring while I was shaving.
He gave me the end-of-the-world stare, long and heavy. Then he burped—dead serious without a blink. I understood it as a declaration.
I got it:
An "I love you," spoken in a guttural language.
I burped back to say, "I love you too," out of respect.
We understood each other.

So yeah, he deserves a chapter. A damn temple, even.

Rocky, you're not just a dog; you're my light on gray days, my raft in the storm. You remind me that life isn't just running, working, yelling, and rinse and repeat.

It's also slowing down, breathing, soaking in the day, and catching those simple shots of pure happiness.

Walking through parks, sitting and staring like dumbstruck lovers—you with your tongue hanging out and me, on the verge of a heart attack because we goofed around in the grass for an hour.

Feeling the wind; lying in the sun (I am pretty sure that's a Stereophonics song); napping without fear, burping without shame, and drooling without apology.

But loving. Loving without a word, loving without limit, without reserve, without bullshit.

You don't have to work to earn your bowl.

You don't need followers to exist.

You're just here, and that's more than enough for me.

That's it.

End of the chapter.

No morals, no lectures, just a dog, a heart, and a holy, sticky, hairy, fluffy, furry lesson of love.

My dog, my hero, my buddy.

This one's for him.

My own brother-in-arms who never deserts me.

Letters to future chefs

And to the apprentices of chaos

⚠ WARNING ⚠

Don't get me wrong—the last thing I want is to sound bitter or resentful or kill the spark in some kid who reads this book or dreams of becoming a chef.

Buddy, if you're thinking about jumping into this madness—or you, reader, if you're wondering whether my brain finally melted from standing too close to the fryer for thirty years—listen carefully.

You better know where you're stepping into before you sign up for this life.

Here are some numbers about this job.

It'll be a bit tedious, but the facts are scary.

Those are kitchen truths

In the United States, kitchens are minefields for mental health.

Between sixty-two percent and eighty-four percent of cooks and kitchen workers say the job damaged their psychological balancc.

Seventy-three percent admit to juggling several demons at once, such as depression, anxiety, and addictions.

Or even better, all of them together.

Burnout isn't the exception—it's the rule.

The numbers on booze and dope are even nastier:

Fifteen percent of kitchen staff drink excessively.

Twenty percent say they've used drugs regularly.
Another twenty percent have been officially diagnosed as addicted—almost double the national average.
And it's always the same poisons every time:
Cocaine to survive double shifts and alcohol to shut down at night or keep going when the tickets pile up. And finally, weed or pills to sleep.
Half the ones drinking during service are sipping from the same bottles they pour for customers.
Alcohol is always right there, within reach—behind the bar, in the walk-in, or in your veins.
It's not a celebration; we don't do it to party or for dancing.
It's a crutch.
We drink to endure.
I'm not shy about admitting I don't touch drugs anymore. But until recently, I had a pretty complicated relationship with alcohol.

So the drop at the end of that road is brutal.
Six percent of restaurant workers admit to having suicidal thoughts each year. It's the second-worst rate of any U.S. industry.
Among cooks, it's thirty-five per one hundred thousand. That's more than double the national average, which is around fourteen.
Among female kitchen staff, it's a full-blown massacre: The rate jumped fifty-four percent in three years.
And around it, the scenery's always the same:
Seventy- to eighty-hour weeks.
Double shifts.

Sleepless nights. Holidays swallowed whole. And zero safety net.
You work against everyone else's clock, sleep when your body gives up, and keep going because there's no Plan B.

The hierarchy is brutal; shouting is the soundtrack, and humiliation comes free with the apron.
Because every plate must be perfect, no matter the cost
The kitchen is a jungle because it runs on sacrifice.
And if you show weakness or fatigue, if you crack or lose it, too bad. You get replaced before your blood dries on the cutting board.
The cult of "keep going no matter what" rules everything.
So you shut up, work, and swallow your pain.
You drink it down, snort it up, or hide in the walk-in.
The pay? A joke.
Wages and instability crush you in the U.S., because many have no healthcare or social protection.
And even experienced chefs are underpaid compared to the pressure they absorb.
Trust me, I know.

Let's cross the Atlantic.
It's been a while since I have worked in France, but from what I read and hear from friends, it's not much prettier.

Gastronomy is on a pedestal, but behind closed doors the reality's the same inferno:
Sixty-five percent of French cooks live in chronic stress.
One out of two in hospitality shows signs of burnout.
One apprentice out of three thinks about quitting before they even finish their training. Or they tap out after a few years of hell.
All this because of the pressure.

And the famous little beer after service is part of the wallpaper, but it's just the appetizer. It stacks on top of everything else: the ten espressos and the few lines to keep going and the couple of drinks to come down. That's the full monty.
Studies show cooks are among the heaviest users of alcohol and cannabis in France. Way above the national average.
It's culturally ingrained.

Suicide is taboo but present.
The Labor Department ranks hospitality as a death zone, among the most exposed trades, right next to police and farming.
Unions speak of rates above the national average, and papers regularly report tragedies—chefs ending their lives in their own restaurants.
You don't hear about them, but we do.

And it's more or less the same working conditions: sixty-five to seventy hours a week, often doubled, days that never end.

Low pay for the majority, especially outside big cities.
And access to substances is immediate: alcohol is everywhere, circulating between kitchens and nightlife.
Every service is a battle against time, against yourself, guests, and never-ending tickets.
Your body eats, burns, cuts, and sleeps debt.
Your head takes the rest.
Yes, health care and unemployment exist; they cushion the fall, but they don't heal a fried brain.
In Europe, protections are better, but the salaries still insult the hours.
You burn your life and go home broke.

That's the truth behind the stars and the Michelin glitter.
They're meat grinders for bodies and minds.
You give everything until there's nothing left.
And when you fall, ten kids are waiting behind you to take your place for half the pay.
Hospitality isn't a job; it's a sacrifice.
You work while the rest of the world celebrates.
And you have the loneliness of coming home to an empty apartment. Or coming home at two am when everyone's asleep.
Your shirt reeking of oil and smoke, your soul running on fumes, and your other half has had enough of waiting.
After feeding a hundred people, you eat a sad sandwich in the dark, in silence. Alone with your scars and your burns.
Over time, very few relationships survive.

There are no exceptions: front of house, owners, cooks—we're all in the same boat.
I'm lucky to have an understanding wife—and she knows that if I did anything else, I'd be even more unbearable—but I'll admit I've come close to disaster more than once.
Your kids grow up without you; you spend their childhood on the other side of the pass.
You miss weekends, birthdays, school shows, and Christmas dinners.
Your social life evaporates; friends go out, and, over time, they disappear.
But you keep sending plates, and your circle shrinks to coworkers and the bottle; your life boils down to the kitchen, drugs, and the comedown.

Compared to that, the office looks like a luxury.
Nine to five, forty hours, weekends off, holidays observed.
You see your kids morning and night, and you take vacations.
Your stress is real but contained, with health insurance and a shrink in reach.
Your addictions are recreational, not vital.
Suicide hovers around thirteen–fourteen per one hundred thousand—far from the kitchen's thirty-four point seven.
Couples hold better, kids grow up with their parents, social lives exist, and you find balance.

So dear customers or future colleagues,
Don't think restaurants are glamorous.
They are not.

Behind every beautiful dish, there's a silent price tag—an entire life of sacrifice and torment. And those lives, they all break the same. For some, in the worse case, it leads to an early grave.
For the others, you trade your life for a few perfect plates—and most days, it doesn't even feel like a choice.

And still...
Since I started in this business, whether in the dining room or the kitchen, there hasn't been a week where I haven't asked myself why I keep banging my head against that wall.
But I wouldn't trade it for anything.
Because nothing gives me more pleasure than this job. Every day, I do what I love most.
I am in my kitchen with my team. Cooking for strangers I'll never see again
I live my passion. And I make a living from it.
Even if it hurts me.
Even if it will eventually kill me. I had two heart attacks.

The days are long and brutal, but they're filled with moments of pure grace.
My daily routine?
Every morning I get to the restaurant first. I'm alone. The silence is almost monastic, with just the fridges purring. The kitchen is immaculate, spotless, and waiting.
I pull a double espresso, sit at a worktable, and contemplate the room with pride. It's a solemn, almost mystical moment.

This is my church.
My menu.
My recipes.
Of course, in a few hours, it'll turn into a battlefield full of noise, sweat, and chaos, but right now, it's mine.
All mine.

You want a magic trick I never get tired of?
You take ingredients, cook them, combine them, season them, and with your hands, your work, and your experience—you create something to eat that gives pleasure to someone.
Simple. Beautiful. Real.
That still gets me every time.

Then there are those small moments.
When a cook nails a dish, you say "good job," and in two seconds, he lights up like a match.
He feels like he belongs.

And once in a blue moon, you get the perfect service.
The house is packed, but there is not a single screw-up. Everything flows. It's fluid, fast, and efficient.
Then you step back and watch your crew move like a single body. Everything is coordinated and locked in. Plates land, hands move, and timing clicks.
And if you focus a little, the noise disappears; you don't hear shouting anymore; you hear unity.
You hear life, music... The music of a kitchen.

That's our symphony.
That's rock and roll.
Then the rhythm takes over; all that's left is cadence, a breath of energy.
It looks like choreography to the millimeter. A culinary ballet.
Sometimes you catch a smirk slipping onto a tight face despite the sweat beading on foreheads—a corner smile, almost hidden.
That's happiness.
Pride.

And then there's the crew.
A pack, with a rallying cry that cracks like a whip.
An engine roaring that sounds like rhythm and fire.
And ♫ *Start Me Up* is all that.
It's raw, nervy, imperfect, but alive.
Richard's sticky riff sticks to your skin.
Jagger's rough voice cuts through the music.
And Charlie Watts' stubborn drums pound the beat like a war drum.
If you add Ronnie Wood, it's four guys united like the fingers of a hand. There were five, but time takes its toll.
Taken one by one, they've got limits, but together they're the fucking Rolling Stones.
A gang of misfits who only work because they play together.
And a kitchen, it's the same thing kid;
It's the same rhythm, the same pulse.
Raw, imperfect, but alive.

A band with a shared fire and a contagious passion.
You can have all the talent in the world—alone, you do nothing.
We fall together; we rise together.
Even the guy you can't stand is your brother during service. Because if he goes down, the whole kitchen explodes.
So you hold the line. You don't quit. You don't leave anyone behind. We lock arms and we support each other because we don't have the luxury of hating.
We do the same job for the same reasons.
We're infected by the same disease.
We all have the same fucking virus.
So we forget it all—the shouting matches and grudges—and we move forward like a welded army.
And the harder it hits, the tighter we get.
That's how we survive.

When service ends, the printer stops spitting tickets, and the last plate leaves. The burners die, and the silence slowly creeps back; then we sit. Not to talk. Not to philosophize... But just to breathe and repay the service with gestures and glances. We share a laugh, a look that says, "We made it."
We're washed out, burnt—but we linger, proud.
And damn, that's real luxury right there.
The one money can't buy.

Being there in that murky end-of-service light, in the truth of a brigade. In that tired glow, among the dirty pans and burnt towels.
That's a moment of grace.
The trade is hard, thankless, and exhausting—but it gives you something nothing else can:
The brutal pride of knowing you didn't cheat. You did not quit.
We gave everything—and we didn't fake a single second. We held the line. Together.
So we raise a glass, keeping one eye on the dish pit and the other on the walk-in. Both filled with a spark despite the dark-circled eyes.
Because we're cooks.
Not heroes.
Not influencers.
Not saints.
Just cooks
And holy mother of fuck... It's beautiful.

And tomorrow?
Tomorrow, we'll do it all again.
Because we can't live otherwise.
Because we don't want to live otherwise.
Because, over time, we don't even know how to live otherwise.
It's our reason for being—our DNA.
Burns and cuts are our war tattoos; our wounds are reminding us every day of the reason we do this. We have chosen this trade, or it has chosen us. It doesn't change a thing.
We have responded to the call.

When the kitchen is clean and everyone bails, I am wrecked, but I am carrying that glorious sense of a job done right, and then comes my sacred nightly ritual.
My procession.
It never changes. It's like a moment of prayer or a meditation.
A minute of gratitude.
I end the day the way I started it. Alone.
I walk through the kitchen one last time. I check the fridges, place my orders, and write tomorrow's prep list.
I sit again at the same table, I have a last glass of wine, and I wipe my knives.
The hood hums above me—the kitchen's still breathing.
I turn off the lights.
There she sleeps.
The fridge motors start snoring—she did have a hell of a day. She is tired.
I am about to leave, full of pride and exhausted, just like her.
I know I won't leave her alone for long because I'll see her again in the morning. And tomorrow she'll spit fire again.
And sometimes she comes back in my dreams; she haunts my nights.
So we'll meet again.
Just before I leave the room, I always tell myself the same thing:
I have the greatest job in the world.

So kid, if you think you're ready for a dramatic, totally blissful epic journey...
A beautiful but brutal, masochistic love story
If you still want to jump in, learn, and survive in this hostile furnace—this blaze—it has to light you from the inside. And if it catches... You're fucked. Because once you start, you'll never stop; you'll burn till the end—like the gods of rock.

And if you're still here, reading this,
You're either destined for the kitchen or just another happy lunatic...or both.
Just like us.
Either way...
Welcome to the club. 

The new guard

There are five rules you can't forget or ignore when you're a rookie in a kitchen.

—Rule Number One:

Keep your mouth shut, watch, listen, learn, absorb like a sponge, do as you're told, and don't be cocky.

Why? because of...

—Rule Number Two:

Be humble. In a kitchen there is always somebody who knows more than you, who is faster than you, and who is more gifted than you are.

—Rule Number Three:

Don't rely too much on technology.

It's good if you have some; it saves you time, but what happens when the KitchenAid doesn't work, when the probe is malfunctioning, or if the timer of your oven is broken?

You have to learn to rely on your eyes, touch, taste, and nose

—Rule Number Four:

Be patient.

Knowing your craft, being trusted to hold a line, and blending in and being part of a crew that is tighter than a latex glove—all this takes time.

Which leads us to...

—Rule Number Five:

Regarding patience, if there is one guy in a kitchen who doesn't have an ounce of it, it's the chef.

I can explain to you, show you, teach you, and be understanding.
But patient? No.
For that particular virtue, go see somebody else.
Why the fuck do you think I have a sous-chef?

That's why I am getting a little worried when people talk to me about the new generation of cooks.
In France, I don't know where things stand, but here... it's complicated.
The newcomers scare the shit out of me because they are completely estranged from those rules.
And they ignore them with a spectacular indifference.
Kids who walk into kitchens today are like backstage celebrities. Headliners in a green room: clean, perfumed, well-groomed, synchronized, and connected.
They glitter, they pose... But the second the heat's on... they crack. And sometimes, shatters.
Because they can't handle the slightest frustration, remark, or pushback.
So we, the old guard, call them the crystal generation.
Personally, I have a nickname for them:
The little princes and princesses of "I want it all, and I want it now." (A song by Queen, maybe)

And that's where Blondie crashes the party with ♫ *Heart of Glass*. Because it's a song that dances on a fault line: bright, fragile, shiny, and a bit naïve.

Exactly like these kids thrown into the storm with their ceramic knives and their embroidered caps. Old-school cooks like me? We're more like Pyrex. Don't shine much, but we take the heat.
The thing is, most of these kids were born here, so there is no language barrier. But there's a gap in values, principles, and conditioning. I am guessing it's generational.
They roll out of culinary school with XXL egos, jackets that have never seen a real rush, and their names stitched in bold on the side.
On that note, let me tell you a cute little story:

At one of the restaurants where I was head chef, I had a partnership with a culinary school in Miami. I'd take interns from time to time.
One day, the director calls me and asks if I can take in a very promising student. A future star, he says. But he warns me the kid is a bit of a thing to manage.
I usually don't take studs with attitude because it never ends well. But I say yes—I'm curious to see the phenomenon.

He shows up in the kitchen the next morning.
My sous-chef and I are still crumpled from the night before—we've got six empty espresso cups each in front of us, and the music is blasting.
The kid introduces himself; I welcome him.
We talk for two minutes. I show him his station, the fridges, the menu, the prep.
Then I get back to work.

Out of the corner of my eye, I see him watching us like we're zoo animals.
I should mention my sous-chef works in a T-shirt and apron. Usually something provocative. That morning it said: "Fuck your diet." He's the only one I allow to skip the chef jacket. The guy's a beast, a workhorse, and I love him.
Yeah yeah, I know—favoritism.
I don't give a shit.

Another thing, in kitchens, we have a knife roll. Five or six knives, a thermometer, a peeler, and a couple of tweezers.
The essentials.
This kid? He pulls out like a small suitcase with wheels. He puts it on the counter. And he starts unpacking. It takes a full ten minutes.
Ten minutes is long. In a kitchen... it's an eternity.
My sous-chef and I look at each other—he's dying laughing; I'm just stunned watching the circus. I am starting to wonder if he's trying too much to make an entrance. Or If he's a traveling kitchenware salesman... or a vet.
I almost tell him the cow's already dead; we are way past surgery. Just cut the rib-eyes from the loin sitting right there in front of you.
But I stay quiet.
I go back to work, and my sous-chef is laughing his ass off.
What now?
Then I see on his jacket his name is embroidered in big letters on the left side in big, proud letters.

At first, I think it's his school jacket. Then I get closer.

Under his name... one word:

Chef.

Chef?

Chef?!

And I get why Keys is laughing—he knows me. He knows I'm about to blow.

What the hell are you chef of, young blood?

But I kept my mouth shut because I've learned there is a new trend.

In the U.S., in TV shows and cooking programs, everyone calls each other "chef." So in modern kitchens, it stuck. Everyone's a chef now. Not just cooks. But servers. Busboys. Runners. Bartenders. Apparently, it's a sign of respect in the new hospitality culture.

Me? It drives me nuts.

At first, every time I heard "chef," I'd turn around and answer:

— Yeah? What's up? To no one, and this fifty times a day.

Turns out it was just a server talking to a bartender who replied to a line cook regarding a comment from the hostess.

A conversation between "chefs."

I tried to explain that where I come from, a kitchen has a hierarchy. There are only two chefs here: my sous-chef and I.

You earn that title. You climb for it.

You carry the kitchen, and you earn the honor of your name on your jacket. Like the army—they're not all generals, right?
Imagine the chaos if they were.
You talk... but it's like pissing against the wind—it rinses your teeth. that's it.
So now there are thirty "chefs" in the restaurant.
And the one getting screwed is my sous-chef—because he's the only one still called *"sous"* something. He's not thrilled.

Anyway.
I ask the kid if he can make a beurre blanc.
He says:
— No, but no problem; give me five minutes. I'll go on YouTube. No need to show me; I've got Internet.
I glance at my sous-chef—I see he's worried about my blood pressure. But I stay calm, and I tell him nicely:
—Listen, kiddo, at school, you've got fifteen minutes to make it with lounge music in the background. The problem is, here you've got four. So by the time you've opened your damn site, the only soundtrack you'll hear will be Table Five screaming because their food is taking too long.
We move on, and I ask him for a béarnaise.
He vanishes and comes back ten minutes later, bitching about the lack of proper equipment, such as a Thermomix.

Quick note: It's a machine where you throw everything in, press a button, and boom—sauce in ten minutes. Magic.
But not in my kitchen.
Here we do it with a wrist and a whisk and a bain-marie. Old school.

I hand him a whisk, a saucepan, and the ingredients.
He looks at me like a fish on a slab.
I bite my tongue to avoid sharing out loud the first thoughts that come to my mind.
—Not so cocky now, huh? Oh, by the way, the Wi-Fi sucks in the kitchen. So good luck with your tutorials. And if you pull out your phone during service, I'll throw it in the fryer.
As I try as much as possible to hide my exasperation, I decide to show him how we do it.
He watches me like I'm a magician.
When I see that, I am forced to ask him.
—What the hell do they even teach you in school?
He explains to me that they have high-end equipment, so they don't need to do this.

And that's when it hits me.
Culinary school doesn't prepare them for real service; it teaches how to operate machines.
But what happens when the machine breaks?
When the mixer dies?
When the oven timer goes off?
What happens when you don't have a probe for the temperature?
They don't teach them how to hold a line.

How to cook under pressure, in noise, and in heat. Here time is of the essence. Urgency is on the menu.

Anyway, long story short, at the end of the service, he asked me how he was doing. Because I had to fill out an evaluation

Eyes locked, I told him, "You still have a lot to learn." But I gave him a favorable report.

I didn't lie; apart from the diva attitude, he had potential. But I also advised him he would probably be more comfortable in a bigger kitchen. So I told him to call me when he would have a little bit more experience. And he did, a year and a half later.

I brought him in, and it went well. He worked with us for a year. But in the end he said he would fit better in a large kitchen doing fancy cuisine. That's when the "I told you so" comes in. Right?

That's why when I read a résumé, I look—but I don't trust it much, because sometimes... You get surprises.

One day, a guy shows up with nothing but his CV and a knot in his gut. His experience? McDonald's and Burger King. That's it.

I'm six-three and not exactly the most sociable and welcoming guy. But I look him in the eye, and I feel something. A spark. A hunger and the will to go further.

Next to him, there was another candidate who was waiting for an interview. Well-groomed. Perfect résumé, Perfect attitude, perfect

references. But too perfect to sweat. Too perfect for me.
So I took the kid who knew nothing. I trained him. He suffered—I won't lie.
He started as a commis, and today he's a sous chef in a fancy place where I once worked.
He had curiosity, integrity, drive, and rage. His talent did the rest. He just had that glint in his eye. I don't take the credit; he doesn't owe anyone. We just crossed paths, and I gave him a nudge. The rest was him.
And that... that gives me a raging hard-on.

On the other hand, I also have turn-offs.
— Do you know French gastronomy? Ever worked in a restaurant kitchen?
— No, but I worked in a school cafeteria and then a retirement home... It's all the same, right? A kitchen is a kitchen?
Yeah... well...no.
Next.

And then we have my favorites, the new influencer chefs.
The ones leaving school wanting to be the nest internet stars... They want to cook without smell, without sweat, without fatigue, without knives, without cracking eggs.
They want to shine, glow, pose, and collect "likes" faster than tickets stack during a rush.
But kiddo, in here you don't win with likes. You win with fire and guts, not with a to-do list shared on Slack.

Forget the Netflix masterclasses.
What do kids want today?
Permanent contracts with no rush and pressure?
Inclusive brigades?
A relaxation room with an essential-oil diffuser, Shiatsu massages, and Feng Shui soundscapes?
Positive feedback every two hours?
I'll give you feedback:
Go get the fucking shallots and move your ass.

Bottom line?
Between the beard dragging on the table, fully tattooed faces, hair down to the kidneys, painted nails...and the inflated egos...hiring here is a circus. Finding the right staff is not that simple.
But sometimes you've got a real one in front of you. One who wants it bad.
And you have to give him a shot.
Because you must never forget where you come from. I was in that same spot starting out. The difference is, I knew I knew nothing... not like them.
But someone believed in me and gave me a chance.
And me... my arms still buzz, my heart still hammers. I still want to show the youngsters that behind their immaculate toques and their Canva resumes... They're going to have to hold the line.
And time will sort out what will happen to them over time.

But don't you worry.

Because on the other side, we have the ones who never tremble, not even the twitch of an eyebrow. Even if they have to whip mayo by hand at one hundred thirteen degrees Fahrenheit in the kitchen in two minutes.
An endangered species...
The old warhorses...
The ones who keep the place standing.
The last resort before everything goes to shit.
The bad seeds.
My favorites.

The old guard

A lot of cooks left Miami and moved a bit north, where rents are cheaper and wages slightly less pathetic.
A good number just got fed up with the business altogether. Most restaurants barely last more than a year. So you're constantly switching jobs, starting from scratch, and of course, with no unemployment benefits. That means no income until you land something else.
We lost a lot of good soldiers.

In Miami, Spanish is everywhere now. In the kitchen, in the dining room. More and more, it's the only language spoken. Some job listings aren't even in English anymore. So if you don't speak it, you're screwed. You look like an idiot.
Which is my case.
Yeah, I know. I've been here over eighteen years, and I still don't speak it. Well... I fake it. I speak some kind of kitchen dialect. And when I don't know a word, I just slap an "o" or an "a" at the end. Communication is a bit slower... But it works. They get me.
Funny how I can switch from French to English in a second without even thinking. But Spanish? That's like quinoa or tofu. It just doesn't go down. Don't ask me why; I have no clue.

Most of the Latino cooks working in restaurants have two jobs.

No split shifts here, so they do lunch somewhere and dinner somewhere else. Hard workers. No question.
What cracks me up is their temper—the shortest fuse on earth.
And God help you if a woman's above them on the line—let's just say they don't love that too much. Machismo is alive and well.
But where it really gets complicated is that Cubans, Hondurans, Peruvians, Colombians, and Venezuelans can't stand each other, and Argentinians only tolerate Argentinians.
So, the kitchen is chaos all day long—shouting, bickering, laughing.
Alive
Exactly how I like my kitchen.

But when it's time to send, when the tickets pile up, they're there. They've got insane pride—they don't let go. No one backs down.
They love to eat, so they ask me about French food and Italian food. We swap flavors and recipes, and I've discovered half of South America's cooking. When it's my turn to cook the staff meal, I'd better not screw up one of their dishes, or I get roasted for a month.
Most of them are in their thirties or older. Trained or not, they show up with a smile, and they get through service without whining or complaining.
I love my crew, wherever they're from.
because we've got the same fire, the same grit.
We're a cheerful pack of lunatics, working in full-volume in a chaotic cacophony.

Regarding the staff I prefer to work with, I won't lie—I like hiring people with experience. But not necessarily for knowledge. I like people who've been through some shit. With scars, folks who know stuff only the pit teaches you. Cooks with thick skin. The kind that can handle pressure, heat, and stress.
In fifteen years in kitchens, I've seen them all, and I've crossed paths with all kinds of cooks.
Good ones, bad ones, hopeless ones.
Some with potential, others... not worth the time.

But four stood out.
They earned my eternal respect and I trust them unconditionally. I hire them wherever I go.
If I had a restaurant, I'd take those four and nobody else. No need.
Four samurai, with whom I'd cook in hell without blinking.
Let me introduce you to my squad of maniacs.
Each has a specialty, each a strategic spot in the kitchen.

The Pastry Chef
Isabel Maria Snurkowski.
"Izzy."
When I first met her, I was... concerned. But she blew me away.
At the time, I needed a pastry chef, and my sous told me he had the right person. I looked at him, skeptical, but he told me not to worry.
Which is exactly when I start worrying.
But I gave the green light anyway.

In the morning she shows up cheerful and energetic.
One weird thing though: whenever I come near her, she jumps, panics, and blushes.
I ask Keys (my sous chef; his portrait is coming) what's up.
He says:
— She's scared and super emotional, and she knows your reputation.
Great. This is going to be fun.

So I tell her I want a "Fraisier" for the dessert of the day. It's a French pastry that looks like a strawberry shortcake. It's a little more sophisticated and a bit more fancy.
Later that afternoon, I go check on it. It looks good. Nice color and well decorated.
I tell her I want to plate it.
She cuts into it, and everything falls apart completely:
The strawberries are sliding one way.
The cream is going the other.
All that's left in the middle are two sad layers of spongy "Genoise."
She stares at me, frozen, bracing for the worst.
Instead of yelling, I look at the mess and burst out laughing, saying:
— What the fuck is that?
She bursts into tears.
I grab her arm, calm her down, and tell her to relax.
— It's just a fucking dessert.

She stops instantly, shocked by my reaction; she didn't expect that. So she regroups, and then she dumps everything in the trash with rage.
I look her dead in the eyes and hammer it home:
— Relax, it's just a fucking dessert.
She goes back to work. And as I walk away, I turn back and say:
— Don't fuck it up.
And I get the best "Yes, Chef" of my life.

From that day on, she understood something essential:
When you know what you're doing, there's no reason to panic.Because cooking isn't just following recipes—it's a feel as well. a mood, a vibe.
And stress kills everything.
"Don't fuck it up" became our line, Our gimmick.
She never messed up another dessert again.
She got so good she got picked up by the Biltmore Hotel. An institution in Miami.
The day she told me she had the opportunity, I said the following:
— Go. Don't hesitate.
She's a gem. I still follow her work.
And yeah... the day she left, I did not say anything, but boy, I felt it.

The Garde-Manger
Krischelle Anne Cordova.
"Pie."
No idea why. Never asked.
A tiny woman. But the ultimate war machine.

Fastest plating I've ever seen. She could fire three or four tables at once.
One flaw... actually two
She had one habit... Even if I were right next to her, she'd scream all the time:
"CHEEEEEF!"
Right in my ear.
So I had no other choice but to scream back:
"YEESS PIIEE!"
Every single time.
The other thing, she'd bring in some neon-colored drink or radioactive candy and asked us to try it. Saying to was from her country. We did want to offend her so we did.
Most of it was awful, disgusting.
Later I found out she did it on purpose.
She picked the worst she could find. And she enjoyed watching us pretend it wasn't that bad.
Yeah... she played us.
She had her fun. So did we.
As well, she was pure gold.

The Line Cook.
Eric Arthur Jr.
A guy with a troubled past. Tattoos on his neck and built like tank. I know he did time for some heavy youthful bullshit; he was in a gang.
But he had a disarming smile, softening his face like a newborn's. You wanted to hug him.
Although I would not recommend trying—he's not exactly the cuddly type.
He went through hell with me, and his torment was beurre blanc.

I demanded it before every service—whisked by hand the old-fashioned way—and it had to hold the entire shift.
I showed him once. Twice. Ten times.
Nothing worked.
Every service—he screwed it up.
Wrong texture, wrong taste, wrong color.
Sometimes it was okay, but ten minutes later the sauce would break.
One month of this. I had to remake his butter every time. I was losing my mind.

One day, I finally decide to change strategy.
As he starts to make the sauce, I move right behind him. I just stand there, breathing down his neck. I don't say a word. I just watch.
He turns his head, look at me, wondering what the fuck is going on. I just stare at him.
He turns back, He holds his nerve while mounting the butter. Once he is done, as the sauce looks decent, I move on.
I make another one just in case without telling him. Better be safe than sorry.
Service hit, and the long-awaited ticket finally arrived:
Whole branzino with beurre blanc.
Once the fish is cooked, they hand it to me, and I start plating.
In the corner of my eye, I see he's sweating bullets, watching me dip into the sauce.
As soon as the spoon goes in it, I see it's silky, smooth, and thick.

I can't help grinning when I put the plate on the window. Because I know what's coming.
I call for service.
Then Eric shows up and stammers:
—The butter... it's okay?
I shoot back, sharp and cold:
— No. It's not okay.
I pause; he's about to implode
Then I lock eyes with him, smile, and add:
—It's perfect.
He nearly cried, and he danced his way back to the line.
He learned something that day: some cooks only shine under pressure.
Him? He needs that edge. When he's relaxed, he screws up. Since he rose to sous-chef in a restaurant in north Miami.

Last but not least, the sous-chef
Monterray Keys.
"Keys."
My faithful lieutenant, my wingman.
Today, he's flying solo; he's running his kitchen in a busy Miami spot.
But at the time, I dragged him everywhere I worked.
I'd call:
—Morning, are you good?
He'd answer:
—Yeah. Where are we going?
His loyalty is real and rock solid.
That's one of the qualities I admire most in a man, in a colleague, or a friend.

A rare virtue… except with the old-timers.
Yep, again.
We trust each other completely.
He knows I work hard; I know what I am doing, and when shit hits the fan, I'm first to jump in. And the more you throw at me, the happier I am.

He's tall and thin with a killer's stare and a charmer's grin. Every time he walks in the kitchen, I hear ♫ *Bad to the Bone* by George Thorogood & The Destroyers.
A greasy hymn announcing he is about to attack the service, like a veteran back for one last rampage.
He doesn't speak loud, but everyone shuts up when he opens his mouth.
Keys isn't a cook—he's a legend in Air Jordans (he can't stand Jordan; I tease him).
Keys doesn't talk about the craft—he grills it.
He enters the kitchen like Clint Eastwood stepping into a saloon. He drops his bag, ties his apron, and stares at his station like a psychopath admiring a crime scene—with appetite.
With him, you know something's going to snap and bleed. The kitchen will smoke, sweat will drip, and there will be meat and fury in the air.
He hits hard and right. I never saw him screwing up a temperature and is always on time.
Old-school. Precise. Deadly.
The best grillman in Miami.
A monster. A pro with a huge pair and not afraid to show it.

We love each other like brothers, but when we clash, it's a bloodbath. We had legendary blowouts.

We can knock out a hundred covers together. Just the two of us. And instead of freaking out, it charges us. We barely need words: a table number, and everything flows. A nod, a look—we know. It's done.
Timing's everything with Keys;
If you're solid, he will trust you; he'll ride with you through hell.
But if you crack, buff, choke, or bail. He'll bury you. He'll smash out five tables at once and leave you gasping, trailing like a fool... and a tiny one.
We're both addicts—to chaos, to music, to food, to brotherhood.
I love that guy like a brother.
I had the honor of being his executive chef for almost eight years in three different restaurants.
I've got the deepest respect and an unbreakable friendship for that world-class pain in the ass.
I wish every chef on earth had keys with them, even just for an hour.

That's my quartet.
With them, I could face any war, any service.
My four magnificent lunatics—if you're reading this, thank you. You saved my ass more than once, and I shined because of you.
My kitchen gladiators.
I miss you all.

And Keys—one last thing: even if you drown your
pasta in ketchup—which makes me lose my shit—
Tell me where and when, and we'll do it again.
We'll fire it up.
Whenever, wherever.

Fuck, I've grown old.
Soft.
Sentimental.
Where's my shovel?

A tale of two

Or maybe three

I've just realized that on top of everything else I am already dragging around, I've developed a split-identity disorder. My brain is like Dr. Jekyll and Mr. Hyde—haunted by two languages, two identities. Two countries, two cultures.
And my heart will always be split between two cities.
Like two sides of my personality. Of my life.
Like Two-Face, the Batman villain.
Like two sides of the same coin.
One city for my heart, one city for my soul.
One city for daytime, one for nighttime.
Like the song ♫ *Paris nights and New York mornings.*
I did not choose this song because it means something specific for me. But it's one of those happy songs. You know the kind; when you hear it, you can't help dancing and smiling.
It has that upbeat vibe that you can feel when you are walking the avenues of Manhattan.
And a hint of sweetness and melancholy that you can have when you are wandering in the streets of Paris.
Listen to this song by Corinne Bailey Rae.
You'll see. It's the right choice for this chapter.

English has become a second skin for me. I work, think, argue, and dream in English. And even at home, we use it because it's convenient; my

daughter was born here, and my wife has been living in the U.S. for more than thirty-four years. So yeah, English is the one I speak, the one I grind with, twenty-four seven.
So I'm bilingual—but not fifty-fifty.
Except when shit hits the fan.
When voices rise, then, French is mandatory.
Trust me, there's nothing like cursing in French. It's rude, brutal, and mean. Imagine verbally butchering somebody but with surgical precision.
Speaking of which,
It's funny how I don't express myself the same way in both languages.
In French, this book has sarcasm, humor, and bite, but also melancholy.
But in English, it's raw, more aggressive, and way more slang, and it has a rage crawling under the fire.
But I wrote this book first in French because that's not just a language. It's my rootstock, my instinct. My refuge. The one that taught me how to say "merde," how to love, how to fight, how to eat, how to take punches, and how to swing back.
I speak English fluently. I can charm, fight, laugh, and even cry in it.
But it's not the same.
English — I use it.
French—I spit it, chew it, and swallow it. I *am* it.
It runs through me.
It keeps me standing.
Exactly like my hometown.
Let's take a closer look at this coin.

Heads: Paris

My identity. My DNA, my accent, my temper.
That city gave me life, raised me, built me up, and tore me down. Taught me how to walk and how to survive. Everything in it is part of who I am.
All that slang, ringing in my ears; that dark humor, sharp as a knife. Sarcasms that are poured in the morning with the croissants. And that arrogance, that is a delicate wine flowing faster than tap water.
The cafés of my teenage years, the pinball machines.
The Sunday markets that shaped my appetite—it all comes from there.

A country where you go on strike instead of working. Where you are cling to that outdated pride that we're the center of the world.
A city that slapped me, kissed me, and spat in my face while serving me the best food on earth.
France is like a pain-in-the-ass girlfriend you can't stand but can't stop loving.
It's my universe, my galaxy.
And I've been suffering in silence for years from missing it—it's an absence that sticks to my bones. It eats my nerves every time when I wake up or when I go to bed.
And every time in between.
When I breathe.
When I take a piss.
When I eat. Especially when I eat.

Since I have been living in Miami, my ritual has always been the same.
I have my morning routine.
Yeah, another one. I am a creature of habit.
I take the dog out—it takes forty-five minutes to pick the perfect tree.
I come back home and have another espresso.
Double this time. Then I sit in front of my laptop and watch French news.
Not for the news. But for the voices. The accents.
The arguments. The chaos.
Because for me, what moves me isn't stability—it's the French catastrophic mayhem.
That's my heritage.
Here in the States, even the mess is organized.
Everything's clean, calibrated, controlled, and dressed up with a smile.

France?
No smile, not even half of it; it's a smirk.
Everything is pure improvisation.
Genius in the absurd.
Mistakes embraced.
Bureaucracy that makes no sense,
People complaining for sport.
Rules nobody understands — including the people enforcing them.
and tax bills that make you want to drown yourself in a bottle of wine.
And somehow... it works.
Everything smells like life there.
The bad weather
The morning baguette is still warm from the oven.

The "Rosette de Lyon."
The corner store is open until midnight with a smile.
The stinky cheese that leaks, and sticks to your fingers
Wines that stain but warm your soul.
In France, recipes aren't suggestions.
You mess with a classic–you go straight to hell.
And that's exactly how it should be.

And the supermarkets... Yeah, I know. It sounds stupid. Trust me, it's not.
If one day you go to France, go to a supermarket; you'll understand, and maybe you'll say to yourself:
—Damn, he was right.
If I went back today — right now — I know exactly where I'd go.
Not the Eiffel Tower. Not some landmark.
I'd go straight to the yogurt aisle in a supermarket. I'd sit on the floor. And probably cry like an idiot.
Because that's where my childhood is stored. ; it's my lost paradise.
I'd trade a kidney for a packet of my childhood cookies, the artillery and ammunition of my early years.
Stuff nobody romanticizes–except when you don't have it anymore.
To Frenchies who would read this: you don't get it because you take it for granted.

Then you have the butcher shops... we dont have those here; they have no idea what they are missing
Jesus.
Walking into a bakery for a fresh baguette and croissants...
Fuck, just writing that brings tears to my eyes.
There are no little shops here where you pick your own veggies and you eat what is seasonal.
I'm shaking just thinking about it.
And to torture myself even more, I picture stepping into a cheese store.
— I stop. That alone could break me.

And then there are the smells and the sounds.
The dampness of the food markets and the chaos of closing time.
Chestnuts roasting on the boulevards in winter, with Christmas lights strung above.
Hot viennoiseries pulled from the oven at dawn.
That fucking truck collecting glass bottles is rattling you awake at five a.m. And being annoyed by drivers leaning on their horns like idiots because a delivery is blocking the street.
That unbearable, sublime mix exists nowhere else.

Le "troquet": the café, but the French way.
Not the polished one you have here but the joint, where you enjoy a coffee while it pours outside.
Standing up at the counter while you read a greasy, blackening newspaper that fucks up your fingers.

I mean the real espresso, no sugar. A juice that would wake up a dead man, not the cup of joe, that watery crap you call coffee here.
Christ, I don't even know how to describe the atmosphere of a joint we call "un café."
The menu is traditional and comforting, with meals from another time.
Two old-timers at the bar trash-talking a soccer coach they've never met.
The owner's bitching because the coffee machine's frothing too much.
And some old guy yelling at nine a.m.:
— Your white wine is corked... like your wife!

And the view from it.
Sitting outside a bistro with a kir (white wine or champagne with red-berry liqueur), listening to the street noise, hypnotized as the city slowly falls into night. Then the lights flicker on, the Seine turns to gold, and the bridges blaze, and you sit there, witnessing the city being reborn.
Strolling the seventh district, or pausing on Place des Vosges in April.
Admiring the elegance of Avenue Montaigne and the Haussmannian charm of the seventeenth-district buildings.
La Place du Tertre, la Rue des Abbesses.
The incandescent beauty of Place de la Concorde.
The Alexandre III bridge.
I'm a Right Bank guy, but the majesty of the Assemblée Nationale brings me to tears.
Saint-Germain, buzzing in spring, and the quiet grace of the Île Saint-Louis.

How the hell can you resist?

Driving through France...
Stopping in some random village.
Getting judged for being from Paris.
Ordering a drink and watching old guys play pétanque.
The coast. The markets. The light. The noise. The silence.
That's life.
It's not just a country.
It's a rhythm.

But above all, what I love isn't just the country.
It's the French.
Their glorious bullshit.
Magnificent.
Genius.
Incomprehensible.
Decadent.
That talent for complicating everything, for creating a messy chaos so beautiful it becomes art.
That biting, insolent, caustic humor.
The kind that stings and scratches but heals.
The kind that tells the whole world to fuck off while being moved to tears eating a dish drowning in sauce.
To understand the French, you first have to look at our plates, our food. The way we do groceries. Being French is bitching in the supermarket line and cursing out the president but crying to Aznavour or Brel at two a.m.

It’s muttering:
—Fuck, this country wears me out...while defending the camembert like it carries your family name.
We don’t respect much.
But we respect pleasure.

Let's flip the coin.
Tails,
New York
I told you about my first trip to New York.
The ones after that went deeper. Hit harder.
That’s where I found my pulse again. My direction.
With my buddy, it became a ritual. Every three months, whenever life started to choke us,
We’d just look at each other—no words needed.
We knew. It was time for our fix. Time for oxygen.
We’d book flights for the next morning. We’d take off Friday morning and come back Monday at dawn. Wiped out... but fully recharged.
Three days of mayhem—walking, eating till our bellies exploded in a frantic restaurant marathon, drinking, and laughing like idiots. With barely any sleep.
And no fooling around with girls.
That was the rule.
No girls. Not the point. Not the need.
It was just the two of us... and our stupidity.

We’d leave the hotel around nine in the morning and disappear into the city until four in the afternoon.

Nap. Shower.
Then at seven, we'd head back out, dressed sharp like kings. We'd leave the hotel dressed like kings and come back looking like crash victims—shirts soaked, hair wrecked, and sometimes missing a jacket. Sometimes missing the shirt entirely.
One night, David lost a shoe in a club—I think it was Bungalow 8.
We staggered back through those half-empty streets where Manhattan breathes differently.
When it's pure magic.
Drunk as skunks.
Alive.
Back at the hotel, we'd crawl back at sunrise, wrecked.
The concierge just stared at us, speechless.
When we left, I am sure he hoped to never see us again

As much as New York City has a soul, a heartbeat, and a voice—Manhattan is the throat that screams. It's dense, brutal, organic, shot through with adrenaline and asphalt.
Nothing about it is postcard material.
Manhattan isn't just Times Square, the Statue of Liberty, or souvenirs wrapped for tourists.
That's a whole different beast.
It's noise, sweat, and sirens.
Ripped garbage bags bleeding onto sidewalks, steam blasting out of the city's veins.
It slaps you, shakes you, grabs you by the balls, and keeps you on the edge of insanity.

It's the only place in the world where I've felt alive
the second my shoes hit the pavement.
The only place that makes my blood boil is just
getting close to it.
That matches the beating in my chest and the fire
in my guts
A chaos that never lies.

New York is Paris's elegance with American
voltage. Cosmopolitan, gothic, greedy, feral.
Shopping at Dean & DeLuca,
The butchers in Brooklyn.
Having dinner at Peter Luger Steak House.
a drink in a dive in the East Village.
And Balthazar—that restaurant is a miracle: a
place where you can eat in Paris without the cost
of the airfare.
Italian delis and food smells on every corner.
Pretzels and hot dogs at every light.
The rumble of the avenues.
Spring, sizzling through SoHo and Bleecker
Street. And those first warm days that remind you
the city is one of a kind
Tribeca in September, when everything feels
almost perfect.
In the fall, the steps of the Metropolitan Museum
of Art are covered in gold leaves, swept by the
wind off Fifth Avenue.
Winter biting your lungs when Central Park is
buried in snow.
Every season is a punch to the gut.
And just like Paris, summer makes it unbearable.

Everything here is too much. Too loud. Too alive.
Harlem. The Financial District. The Brooklyn Bridge.
And all the backdrops from the movies that raised me—Once Upon a Time in America, Wall Street, and a hundred more.
Walking down the street and running into Al Pacino.
Stopping for a drink at The Peninsula New York bar and having Michael Keaton casually ask you for a napkin.
Grabbing a bite at the Four Seasons Restaurant with John Travolta sitting at the next table.
This city brought me back to life.
How can you not love New York?
Manhattan is irresistible.
It's poetry in motion.

And here's the tragedy.
That fucking coin—I'll keep it, but only as a memory and in my pocket.
I won't go back to live in Paris or New York.
Not because I don't love them—on the contrary, I love them too much.
I'll go back, sure, but only as a visitor. A tourist.
I don't have the strength to be a soldier there anymore.
But like a past crush, you have to let it go.
And it's time to let Eric Clapton end this chapter with ♫ *Old Love,* from the unplugged album.
It reminds me of the sadness when you say goodbye and need to move on for your own good, for your own sanity.

Because I've given enough, I have to leave them both behind me. I don't want to end up hating those old loves of mine.
I'm tired and burned out. I need a break from the commotion.
I want a new light and the carefree vibe of the countryside.
I want peace—but the real kind.
The one you find in the south of France.

In Provence.
The calm, the raw sun, the shade of plane trees, and the terrace of a bar where laughter is loud.
Rosé wine, cooling your throat.
Markets that reek of garlic and ripe tomatoes.
Summer nights that last longer than life itself.
Landscapes that wash your head clean.
People who don't take themselves seriously with that accent that sings and stings at the same time.
The mistral wind driving you mad, the scent of lavender, and olive trees dancing in the sky.
A small village, forgotten by time, with these voices rising higher than the church bell.
The sea in the distance. Crickets at night.
There I have found my new love affair.
My new life.
One that doesn't swallow me whole but lets me breathe.
After all these years of war, noise, and flames, I don't want to scream; I just want to exist in peace and harmony.
I've earned it.
It won't be the warrior's rest but a transition.

Not a resignation.
Not an escape.
Not a raging river, but a life like a long, quiet stream.
Home. Among my own.
Turn on the TV and stumble upon an old movie, a Delon or a Belmondo. Maybe a Louis de Funès or, even better, an old Michel Audiard flick.
And let time do the rest.

And one last thing.
My wife always tells me the following:
— You're not just French; you're a franchouillard.
Not a compliment—fuck it, I'll take it.
And she's right, and I'm proud of it.
It's my medal.
My badge of honor.
Yes, of course, my country has changed. The world changes. Everything changes.
Even me.
But what doesn't change is the spirit.
I can't help noticing how people look at us like idiots wherever we go.
"Ah, you French people..."
Yeah, well, you know what?
We're proud of being this stupid and stubborn.
For us, it's a badge of distinction.
Our own Medal of Honor.
And yet, we still do things with taste and class—food, fashion, art, industry, architecture, cooking, and even sweet talking.
Baby, we invented this bullshit.
I rest my case.

Not too bad for a bunch of morons, right?
So from France with love, with a smirk and a shit ton of sarcasm.

The calm before the shitstorm

For once, I am going to start the chapter with the music. Because it sets everything.
And I'll introduce David Gilmour to ride along—and not by accident.

Because ♫ *Between Two Points* is a clear line, thin and fragile.
Then slowly, a rise—a quiet, discreet climb that won't let go, like a suspended breath. And at the end... that solo. Not fireworks, but a demonstration; not loud, but brutally elegant.
It's a track with no showing off, no glitter. Dripping melancholy and exhaustion like a rope stretched to the snapping point.
Every note weighs, and every silence counts.
Like a kitchen at the end of service, when the noises die one by one. When the bodies are worn and fatigue sets in... But the love of the craft, of the kitchen, of the people—keeps beating under the noise.
I chose that track because it doesn't try to impress. It walks with you like a shadow. Wraps around you. Lets you think and lets you drift.
And that's exactly what I needed.
A silent scream hurled into the void.

That's what this chapter is.
That's the vertigo of the choice, the beauty of the doubt when it settles in. It does not leave you in peace, but it forces you to think about tomorrow.
And that's exactly where I'm at.

In between.
Between what I am and where I am going.
Between two countries, two choices, and two lives.
Two versions of me.
Two versions of us.

I walked through the flames of addictions and defeat, screw-ups, losses, and tiny wins. They forged me.
But I'm still here. Not insane—not entirely—but definitely dented.
All those years in this industry wrecked my body.
And I'm not twenty-five anymore. Which means I take longer to recover, to sleep, and to absorb the hits.
I am less explosive. Slower. But I am sharper because of the skills and the knowledge I have collected through all those years.
I am less stupid and less on edge. I am more willing to enjoy the years ahead of me.
because I know what I'm doing. And I am in a good place in my life.
But I am not kinder, not more likable. Not nicer, not more "pleasant."
That? Don't hold your breath. Not a chance.
I still got the rage and the hunger.
The engine may be secondhand, but it still growls.
So I want to keep going—just differently.
I want less, but mostly, I want better.
And I know damn well what I don't want anymore.

Fuck the factory kitchens.
Screw the weekends that never existed—erased in the name of service.
No more ninety-hour weeks cranking out plates for people who don't even taste what they eat.
I am dropping that shit.
I'm done with overpriced brunch culture.
TripAdvisor clowns and bearded influencers.
Owners preaching margin over flavor.
Burnouts dressed up like hero stories.
Done with Netflix chef egos and cooking competitions turned testosterone theater.
Ego wars and self-loathing.

I'll keep the rest though—the stuff that burns right.
The passion.
The discipline.
The taste and the love for a job done right.
The simple gestures and old recipes.
Garlic, sizzling in a hot pan.
That tiny smile from a guest at the first bite.
I'll keep my bad faith and my rants.
My tenderness, buried under the testosterone.
My stupidity. It keeps me moving and keeps me from drowning in boredom.
And I'll keep the itch to pass it on.
So the old bastard teaches the young bastard so he doesn't grow into a bigger bastard.

And now? What's next?
Honestly? I don't know.

Maybe I'll learn how to live the way I learned how to cook my favorite dish. —carefully, patiently, with respect.
I want meaning. Small. Real.
A human-sized kitchen and a dining room full of smiles, not followers.
A joint like an acoustic guitar: no tricks, raw and imperfect, just something that rings true.
Where we talk, laugh, eat, and mop up sauce—basically just the raw pleasure of cooking and sharing it. Nothing more.
But not nothing at all.
Fuck no.
I won't go out like that.
It won't end like that.

Maybe a little bistro in a small country town. A side street, a flowered terrace.
A checkered tablecloth and a menu that shifts every week.
My dog at my feet, sniffing the special, waiting for his bowl, drooling.
Watching my daughter laughing while devouring a plate of profiteroles in seconds.
My friends at the bar, pouring the apéritif.
My wife, sitting on the terrace, throwing me the look—sharp, loving, but annoyed—because I sneak out to toast with them, a glass of rosé in my hand.
Life.

Either way, the moment has arrived.
It's time to say thank you.

To those who backed me and carried me.
Those who betrayed me, those who didn't believe.
The bastards who made me move forward the hard way.
Those who smiled, those who trashed me.
Those I pushed, those I inspired.
The incompetent pricks I fired—or the lost souls I shoved back on track.
And thanks to me, too—me, the stubborn prick.
I never gave up or let go, even in the worst moments.
When it all went to hell, when it seemed hopeless.

This life and the craft taught me a lot of things, but one specifically stands out.
As a parent, I have something to share. It's not advice, but a plea.
If one of your children have a passion, something in life transcends them.
Encourage them.
Let them live it, breathe through it, and shiver for it.
And if one day they tell you they want to be a chef, I promise, it isn't that bad.
I know very few jobs that make you feel that alive.

We are getting close to the end. So, let's take a pause. A French one.
One that is a little classy and a little messy at the same time. A breather, like a palate cleanser between courses.

Because I want to thank you as well for hanging in and walking that mile with me.
We've been through my past and my present. And you saw I have had my share of mistakes. I collected them like stamps, but they brought me here.
I failed many times. But I never allowed those failures to define me.
This is an ode to life and a relentless fire.
And just like for a recipe, when you screw up, you refire, you re-plate, and resend.
And you move on.
I'm the poster child for redemption. I was good at nothing, bad at everything, and doomed to a questionable future. But I hauled myself out of the pit. I took the hits, sweated, worked, and hung on.

Today I'm a chef.
Every time I think about it, I can't help smiling.
A tired one, yes. But a proud one. The victorious and satisfied kind.
Satisfied, because I was born with a solid gold spoon in my mouth—but it was full of shit. So, I did what I do every day at work:
I changed the menu.
And victorious because I owe my survival to the love of this craft, to my wife, my kid, and my dog.
And to my shitty temper.

So one last piece of advice to every apprentice of chaos, to every kid who wants or dreams to be a in this trade:

In this job, in the beginning you need to shut your mouth and clench your ass.
And if someone is rubbing your nose in your mess. Just admit you fucked up and learn from it and rise again.
But most importantly, fight with every bone in your body. Because there will be times when you will be tempted to drop it, to give up. You'll feel helpless, stuck, discouraged, or burned out at the end of the road.
Try to resist this urge. Don't take a decision on the spot that you might regret for all your life.
Instead, try to refocus and cool down.
But keep a whiff of revolt in the back of your mind. And use it when you need it to keep your feet on the ground, and your head above water.

It happened to me.
And that day I tried to remember why I picked this job in the first place. But as I was still struggling to gather my thoughts, I heard that anthem rising. And it helped me when I needed it the most.
It was not a slow dance, not a lullaby. Not a caress.
But a thrilling, haunting, and deafening track.
I knew that guitar, Richards' riff, sharp as a razor slash to the throat.
Then a grave, raspy voice, cracked by dope and endless nights, grabbed me by the collar—that was Jagger.
It was—♫ *Gimme Shelter*. A hymn of war, love, thunder, and fire. And it lit the fuse again.

Today I hear again. It sounds like an air raid siren. An alarm.
Because I know calm never lasts; relief is just a lie we tell ourselves to survive.
For me, today it's more than a song; it's a countdown.
Peace is over; it's the moment of truth.
The endgame.
This is usually where choices are made.
Resolutions are taken. Big decisions that change the course of lives.
And that's exactly where I'm at. I need to make a drastic change...but not for anybody else but my clan.
Because I am stuck between a ♫ *rock and a hard place* (another Stones piece).
Rot away under the Florida sun...or feel something again, with my people, back home in France.
Head high. Blade in hand.
I feel a storm brewing. It's time for one last stand as a testament to this crazy life and maybe write a new chapter.
I still have time.
Just not today.
Tomorrow, maybe.
But tomorrow doesn't wait.
And fuck it... neither do I anymore.
I can take it anymore.
It's been twenty years. I've given two decades of my life to this country.
They flew by in the blink of an eye, and I loved every minute of it, but I am done.

I just don't want to leave here anymore.
Would I stay in the US?
Would I settle somewhere else?
I am not even sure. I don't understand this country anymore. Something shifted. Maybe it's just Miami that wore me out.
Maybe the world changing too fast for me, or maybe it's just me. I reached an age where it's getting harder for me to adapt.
So I need to be there when I have landmarks. Ground marks under my feet.
I need to go back where I fit, or at least where I belong.
I know things there have changed as well out there. But it's shifting in a slower way.
We are the old world after all. Always showing reluctance to change, holding on to our pace and our way of life. Stubborn, flawed, but alive.
No matter what.
Just like me.
It's time to grab what's left of my courage and cut ties.
I know what I have to do.
I want to get the hell out here.
Only one problem...
I have to convince the family.

Last order

I look at my chef jackets the way a boxer looks at his old gloves—worn out, stained, faded.
They still carry the marks of the fight.
Mine doesn't smell like dried blood but fire and sweat.
It's more than a uniform. It's armor.
I look at my hands—beat up just the same.
His, from punches and uppercuts.
Mine, from blades and burns by a four hundred-degree oven and burning oil. By carrying plates, trays, pots, and pans for three decades.
Our bodies tell the same story: too many hours, too many fights.
I remember my victories: against drugs, against emptiness, against failure. And the best one—the one that defined me—I won it in the kitchen.
Losses? Yeah... those ones stick. They sit under your skin. They don't go away.
Like him, I remember my last fight.
It wasn't pretty. I got my ass whooped. I am still groggy.
I wasn't fighting a chef or bad service. It was something worse, stronger, more ruthless.
Exhaustion. Boredom. Wear and tear.
The insecurity, the survival mode, the urgency of living in a city that keeps punching you—slowly, methodically—until it eats you alive and makes you forget your dreams. Make you sleep with your eyes open.

And I was against the rope, stuck in my corner,
legs shaking, struggling to stay on my feet.
At the end of the last round, I was empty, beat up.
But not ready to throw in the towel yet.
I knew I could not win, but I needed to go the distance.
So yeah, I will give punch for punch; I won't go down without a fight.
And...
And?
Oh, the hell with it!

Let's be honest—this chapter bores you as much as it bores me.
Really, who gives a damn?
After all the crap I've thrown around, since it's the last chapter, I wanted to end on something motivational and inspiring. But now that you know me a bit, you know that's not my style, not my thing.
Honestly? It's not working. I can't do it;
And let's face it, it sucks; it's crap.
So screw all the boxer metaphor bullshit.
Speaking of which,
Rocky II is my favorite film. I tell you that because that's where the dog's name comes from.
Didn't see that coming, duh?
Ok so I'm cutting the crap right here.
That's not my thing.

So why am I telling you this?
No idea.
Maybe because it's late.

I just got back from work. I'm exhausted. Hungry. But there's no way in hell I'm cooking anything tonight. I've had enough.
So I poured myself a big glass of wine and sat down in front of my computer.
Because on my way home, I was thinking about how to end this book. And I was stuck between two moods:
♫ Street Fighting Man and/or ♫ Eye of the Tiger.
And then it hit me.
Simple.
No fake wisdom. No soft landing.
I'm not ending this on some sugarcoated, polished crap hoping to sound like the nice guy of the week or a saint.
I'm going to end it on madness, on hope, on grandiloquence.
Something loud and over the top.

I'm going to finish with U2.
Obviously, because what's more uplifting, more electric, and more full of life than ♫ *Where the Streets Have No Name*?
This song leaves you in total ecstasy, complete bliss. The raw energy and the power of that song are like an incandescent light.
It's a climb, a celebration of life. An electric prayer.
A sprint toward something you might never reach, the perfect service, the perfect plate—but you

chase it anyway because without that, you're dead inside.
The guitar intro from The Edge grabs your soul.
The drums of Larry Mullen Jr. kick you back on your feet.
And Bono's voice... rips your chest open to let the light through.
And you finish breathless but pumped, charged up, wired, and ready to take on the world and dance butt-naked in the street.
It's not a hit. It's a revelation.
A call. A horizon. A promise.
It's a way out, an exit.
And it's mine
I'm walking out on this track.

I tried to write a book that breathes and lives. To give an idea of what this job feels like.
To share my passion. My exhaustion. My feelings.
To throw out my guts and my truth.
But to make a statement full of optimism for once,; it isn't over till the fat lady sings.
Nobody's doomed to ruin their life.
But you've got to fight; you've got to live. Laugh, feast, drink, bitch, yell, vent, and even rant. If you have to. Trust me, it feels good to let it all out.
And love. Love madly, deeply, head over heels.
Love stupidity and craziness.
Love your friends, your job, and your life.
And say it—to your wife, to your kids.
Don't be afraid or concerned of what people think or say about you.
What is that famous quote from Oscar Wilde?

"Be yourself, because everyone is taken."
So don't be afraid to fail or to crash. Just do or don't. Don't try.
Only the ones who don't do anything never make mistakes.
Learn to say yes and accept saying no—to others and especially to yourself.
And stop lying to yourself, because nothing lasts.
We're all just passing through.
We all know how it ends—we're all on the same damn train, headed to the same hole in the ground.
Maybe not hell, maybe not a septic tank.
But hey, might as well laugh before the first shovel of dirt hits.

People freak out when you talk about death.
Me? Not really.
The Grim Reaper doesn't scare me more than that.
Don't get me wrong, I'm not thrilled about it—the later, the better—but I'm at peace with it.
Not exactly cheerful, I know. Oh come on, nobody died. Yet.
Joke aside, what scares the shit out of me is being erased. Disappearing. The idea is that once you're gone, it's like you never walked this earth.
Maybe that's why people have kids—to leave a trace.
But the thought that, on a Monday (why the fuck Monday?), the day after I'm gone, people will still bitch in traffic, do their grocery shopping, order Uber Eats...

Business as usual.
That pisses me off.
Yeah, it's selfish. Egotistical. Whatever.
At least I admit it; at least I own it.

I have thought about the end. More than I should have to tell you the truth.
Life's been generous to me, but it has kicked my ass hard, too. And I never asked for much, but I have one wish—just one:
To go before my wife, my daughter, or my dog.
Because if any of them leave before me, that's the first nail in my coffin.
By the way, like many of you, I wonder sometimes, what's next? Is there anything else?
I'm not religious and don't have faith. I don't believe in heaven or reincarnation. I like the idea because the real nightmare is not the box—it's the void.
Will I be able to drift like smoke, drop by for a ghost beer, and flip a cosmic middle finger?
Or is it curtains down and eternal nothingness?
That's what rattles me.
I guess the only thing I truly fear is being bored for eternity. I think that it's the worst thing that can happen to me.
You there, whether in heaven or hell—AC/DC said it wasn't that bad. They made it sound fun enough —But there is nothing. It's dull.
Seriously? That's it?
Maybe we should hang around this idiotic world a bit longer. At least as much s we can. Or allowed to. Just in case.

Come on—who hasn't imagined their own funeral?
Who shows up?
Who fakes crying?
Who whispers "good riddance" while scrolling their phone?
The only thing I know is I don't want a sad circus. The few funerals I've been to were colder than a morgue. I want the opposite. I've had one hell of a life, so I want music and booze. I want smiles and filthy jokes.
You know, the kind like
— Well, at least he finally quit drinking.
I've laughed too much in this life to make my last exit a tearful tragedy.
Just one thing, please: make sure the eulogy's not awkward. Don't make me sound like a saint.
I was kind to the ones I loved—the others, not always.
Am I going too far? Maybe.
Oh, by the way—who's picking my outfit?
I don't want anything fancy—just something comfortable. But no damn sweatpants; I hate that shit. My wife will decide.
Just one favor... Leave the casket open—because when or if I go before my dog, I want him to see I didn't bail on him; I didn't abandon him.
Tell him I had an appointment I couldn't cancel or something to do that will take me forever to finish.

Then, the eternal dilemma: location, location, location.
Buried? Hell no. The thought of staying too long in one place always bothered me already alive.
Cremated, I'm a chef—being roasted fits. But damn it...
— Well done? Seriously?
That goes against everything I've ever cooked.
But what about the ashes? Scattered somewhere?
Sounds like a good idea. To be out there for eternity
If my wife keeps them? I'll probably end up in a drawer or under the mattress. At least if one day she forgets where she put me. She can have a little fun with me. Hide-and-seek, even in death.

Funny how many details there are to settle.
For example, if there is a wake, can I pick the menu in advance?
For fuck's sake, who's going to cook? Please—no quinoa, no tofu, no smoothies.
Will there be a bar... Hey, what about a happy hour? So my wife at least can say I left her with a little something.
Oh, and the music? Rock, obviously.
Now that I think about it, I'll probably have to go into a church. Shit, there's no way around it this time.
Yeah, it's dark. But I don't want my family to be crushed.
I just want them to know I'll be with the ones I miss.

I'll play guitar with Prince and talk music with Bowie and George Michael.
Talk shop with Anthony Bourdain.
Laugh with Carlin, Richard Pryor and Robin williams.
Tell my uncle everything I did.
Finally I feel better; it looks like I am going to buy after all.,

Girls—look at the bright side! I'll be closer to your hearts than I've ever been. Right there, haunting you. Yeah—I'm not done annoying you.
And Peggy, I'll wait for you patiently. Take your time; when you're ready, I'll be there. On the other side.
And hey, I just realized something that cheered me up. Sinatra will be up there—so as soon as I get there, at least someone will tell me where the bar is.

Alright, enough bullshit.
This is a moment of grace—let's not ruin it.
Turn on the stereo and play the song.
Crank it up and close your eyes.
I'll do the same; I'll shut the fuck up.
I'll kill the gas. Clean the kitchen and wipe my blades.
Turn the volume up till the walls shake.
There you go; it was the last call, the final order.
And my last will, all wrapped up. Notarized by publication for posterity.

Oh, wait, you can stick around for a minute—I've
got one last thing to tell you before we part ways.
and one stupid idea to pitch.
In the meantime, I'm going to grab a drink.
Should I print you the check?

Dream menu

I am outside the restaurant, smoking a cigarette before the service.
In the streets, April's acting like a diva.
I love this treacherous month, when spring hasn't picked a side yet—life pushes through everywhere while winter still clings to the eaves.
It's sunny one day and squalls the next. Tonight a freezing rain is coming down sideways, almost like sleet. It can't decide between water and flakes. It almost looks like snow.
The wind cuts through in bursts. The air carries a scent of renewal... and of longing.
I am going back in; I want to make sure that everything's ready.
I take a peek at the reservations; they look promising for an opening night.
The menu's set, and it looks like me—nostalgic, old-school, no bullshit, no compromise.

APPETIZERS

• Garlic butter escargots
• Country pâté & rillettes
• Celery rémoulade
• Leeks vinaigrette
• Herring & potatoes
• Frisée with bacon lardons and poached egg
• Whelks / shrimp with aioli
• Eggs Mimosa (yeah, ours hit harder, no garlic, but shallots)

- Fish soup, rouille, garlic croutons
- Vol-au-vent

MAINS

- Beef bourguignon
- Veal blanquette
- Ribeye, béarnaise, potatoes gratin
- Roast leg of lamb & flageolets
- Ham and endive gratin
- Roast chicken & mashed potatoes
- Steak tartare
- Dover sole meunière
- Seafood tower
- Mussels marinière
- Sweetbreads & grilled kidneys

DESSERT

- Aged cheese board
- Floating island
- Paris-Brest
- Grand Marnier soufflé
- Pink praline tart
- Lemon meringue tart

Voila! Not very trendy, I confess.
But I didn't become a chef to serve boiled vegetables and sad salads.
I cook food that rattles the soul. With butter, cream, sauce, and stock. And flavor.

In the dining room, the team is just resetting the table where we had the staff meal. It was not light, and there were no pitchers of tap water.
We smashed a proper duck Parmentier with a frisée covered with garlic and a glass (two, I think) of red wine.
We needed it.
When I am back in my lair, I scan my mise en place and wait for service to kick off. I'm nervous but confident.
I look at my kitchen—we're proud of what we pulled off. I say "we" because Peggy walked it with me the whole way.
I check the last details.
Tonight is not the night to fuck up.

In the dining room the stereo is blasting a cheesy playlist made of eighty's hits and French classics—guilty pleasure stuff. The kind that makes people smile without knowing why.
I hum along. It calms me down.

I watch a server walking to greet a table, laughing. He's going through the menu, talking about the specials, and dropping a few jokes.
I know his schpiel by heart. I've known him for years. I watched him work. He's hilarious, a nut job, but a pro. That's why I hired him.
—Hey guys, welcome. Let's warm up with a little foreplay. Folks, should we start with an aperitif?
— So, for Madam?
— "A what? Vegan gluten-free low-calorie option?"

Sorry, the chef tried it, but it pissed him off. So—no. Here, we don't *fuel*. We eat.
— And for the gentlemen? Ah, he's already smiling. He picked a shared starter, his appetizer, his main, and his dessert.

Next table.
— Good evening, welcome!
— Do we have organic wine?
— I am afraid not. We don't do that here, but I've got beet juice if you're desperate.

Next table
Oh look—tourists. Americans. Cool.
— Welcome, Madam. Nice to have you both here. What will it be?
— A starter, main, and dessert. Damn, she knows what she's doing.
— And for your husband?
— A ribeye? Sure. Well done... We're off to a great start. And what? Do I have ketchup?
— Out!
—Just kidding. Madam, you may stay. You, sir, are out.

The room is full, but the pace is easy; the guests aren't in a rush, and people want to linger, sip wines between courses, and swap stories. Tables talk to each other. Faces glow, smiles shine.
In the kitchen, tickets spit from the printer in a steady rhythm.
The place smells right—old-school recipes, tradition. Authenticity.

Every now and then… I feel something; a shadow or a presence next to me. Like the old ones are watching. Putting their hands on my shoulder, saying, "You got this."
Peggy comes in, all smiles…saying she' starving but complains she doesn't know what to eat.
"Everything's too rich."
I laugh.
"Don't worry, I'll make you something later."

Service winds down.
I head out; I step into the dining room to thank the guests and say hello. We laugh, we talk, and we share and savor this untamed perfect slice of happiness.
The room carries something unreal, like time got suspended. For a breath, it's just us, and the everyday crap doesn't exist. The world's on pause.
I go back to my kitchen; I cook something for my wife. When it's tel her her food is ready, she insists on eating in the kitchen. We both like the vibe of the evening, and we want to enjoy every second of it.
We debrief the service. What was fine, what went wrong, comments about the dishes.
I'm not hungry. In fact I'm full. I gorged myself on smells and flavors all night. But out of greed, I cut a couple slices of cheese with that I nibble with bread and a splash of red.
Once we are done, I wipe my station down, but I still feel that presence, but this time, it's closer, more real. I'm not alone; I feel watched.

It's rocky; my dog's there, stretched out in the office off the kitchen, just his head poking out like he's keeping an eye on me from the corner.
We lock eyes; I nod and smile to let him know everything is ok. To tell him I love him as well.
We're good—side by side. We are never apart.

The last tables pay, and the guests leave.
The commotion of the closing starts; chairs scrape, doors sigh shut, and the dining room exhales.
But I stay in the kitchen. Alone.
Silence falls, light as snow, and the hum dies away. What's left is the soft breath of cooling fans and the low purr of the fridges.
I wipe the burners, but the garlic and veal stock perfume hangs on, like music that refuses to fade.
The night leans in, saturated with memory.
Even though I am in a good mood, a wave of melancholy slams me.
I think about my life, my screw-ups, and my dumb choices. The years that led me here.
Every sacrifice, every scar it took to get to tonight.
The efforts, the relentless work, and all the people who walked with me all along that chaotic journey. The friends and maniacs I picked up along the way.

Suddenly sadness crashes the party brutally. I feel a void, an absence.
I think of my ghosts—those who aren't here, those I wish I could share this with.
I chew on old memories.

Her. Reading at her kitchen table—her favorite thing in the world—and eating an apple.
Him. Smiling like an idiot, turning everything into a joke.
I close my eyes, straining to hold on to the sound of their voices before it fades.

A melody on an acoustic guitar threads in and hangs in the air. I resist, but the grief sits and crushes my chest.
Prince's voice tears through the empty kitchen, singing of sorrow and a broken heart.
I open my eyes, wet and full of tears, and for a heartbeat, two soft, still silhouettes appear in the doorway.
In the half-light, faces form, slowly shaping out of the dark.
My grandmother and my uncle stand there.
Silent. Still. Floating. Smiling.
I don't move. I just... Look, and I smile back.
I twitch a hand—awkward, unsure—like a wave, not even sure why.
Maybe to give them the farewell life denied me.
I say goodbye.
Then they vanish.
Like mist on glass.
They dissolve.
I cry, overwhelmed.

So I let the sadness do its work, and the melody pours through me.
All that remains is that hymn of loss that knows exactly where to land.

A song that knows everything, that peace is just a word.
I know the grief will return, untouched. Intact.
Nothing has erased it. The ache never leaves.
The wound stays stubborn, deep, and hardheaded. It settles in my head like an echo I can't mute.
How do you heal a hurt that never fades?
A pain that never ends?
A wound that won't close,
A love that won't thin.
You go on with it; you live with it. I know I'll carry it to my last service.
To my last breath.
I turn off the burners and kill the lights.
The smell lingers. The presence stays.
Whether they return or not, from now on, they know where to find me from now on.

I step outside.
A fine rain chills my cheeks.
The grief has set in—frozen somewhere under the skin, in my heart, and deep in my soul.
Yet I smile, because I am happy. And I realize that it is true;
♫ *Sometimes It Snows in April.*

Oops.
Looks like I just wrecked the mood again.
Damn.
It's ok, it's almost time for us to say goodbye anyway.

Kitchen Is Closed

We started in rage and fury; we're going to finish in calm, in elegance, and in softness.
I needed tenderness. Dimmed light.
Not an explosion, but a sigh.
Because this epilogue isn't a light going out; it's just a whispered truth.
So let's play something that awaits you in the shadow, like an ambush.
Something that catches you before you fall. That grabs you by the heart.
A song that wraps its arms around you without judgment. Something that you can listen to without prejudice.
C'mon, right there. I just gave you a hint.
Because for that kind of piece of bravery, that kind of moment, there's only one man:
George Michael.

And ♫ *Waiting (Reprise)*—that's what it is.

A hand reaching out in the dark.
It does not sound like a victory or a resurrection—it's just a song that gives you the strength to stand after the storm.
It's the soundtrack of the aftermath.
When you've burned, screamed, loved, and fought.
When you've emptied your guts and you're still standing.
That's all there is to say.
Not much more to add.

Except a final thank you to the people this book is dedicated to:

I wrote it for her. For them.
And for all of you, the marbled ones in kitchens and the clients.

For Peggy,
My wife, my light, my patience, my hurricane.
The one who picked me up when I acted like a smart-ass.
Who waited when I was being a fool.
Who saved my skin without making it a show.
Who loved me, despite myself, and whom I love like my life depends on her.
And trust me, it does.

For Rafaelle,
My daughter.
Beautiful as the dawn and tender as the night.
My princess. Kind and sensitive—too much—and funny.
Who goes through life singing ...too much, as well.

If I'm honest, they all deserved better.
But they got me.
And I love them like crazy.
Even though I know I disappointed them sometimes, often even.

For Rocky, my dog.

The only one who doesn't judge me even when I talk to myself, who listens to me yell without blinking.
And sometimes I feel like he actually gets me.
He spends half of his life in the kitchen, like me.
He snores in it, like it's his own.
That tender look and that smile make it hard to resist him.
Yep, I've got a dog that smiles.

For Claude,
My stepdad.
I remember what you told me one day: life is only worth living if it feels like a dream.
Well, here it is—I made them true and lived mine.

For Rosa and Jef,
I miss you painfully.
I wish you could've met my wife, my kid, and my dog.
Laughed with us and lived this a bit longer.
Life had other plans.
That fucking bitch.

For David.
My buddy.
Thirty-five years of laughter, of backing each other up. Of getting lost and finding our way again.
Stupid stunts, sleepless nights, and memories funny enough to dislocate our jaws.
The kind of buddy you never forget, the kind of brother you choose.

One day, we'll meet again over wine and a cured meat platter, remembering dumb movie lines that used to make us howl with laughter.
And we'll crack up till we choke, just like before.

For Agathe, my goddaughter.
I live eight thousand kilometers away, always too far, too late, too busy, or too absorbed.
But you're there, in a corner of my heart.
One day, we'll catch up.

For Pascal Oudin,
A lunatic, a psycho, a boss, and a chef like they don't make anymore.
He gave me my chance and drove me nuts.
But he taught me the meaning of work and effort and how to keep the wheel steady when everyone else is bailing.

For Fabien Chalard and Julien Géliot,
Real guys, demanding, generous, and respectful of the craft. And a sense of humor that never fails.
I worked for them in Lyon and Miami, and I walked away with respect and gratitude.
You don't meet guys like that every day in this industry.

For Ed Carter,
whom I worked for in Palm Beach.
A kind, caring, delicate boss.
True elegance, a real gentleman.

And for all of you —

all the lunatics, the crazy souls in chef's jackets.
The night-eaters and the line junkies.
The burned-out ones who keep going.
The veterans who gave everything and the kids who still haven't understood a thing.
The loud, the loyal, the lost.
The maniacs, the geniuses, the broken.
Those I made laugh, cry, and scream—sometimes all at once.
Those I carried... or kicked out.
Those who pissed me off and those who gave me back some faith in humanity.
I've loved you, hated you, sometimes both—but I never ignored you.
Because that's what a kitchen is: a madhouse of souls, blades, and flames.
There is no room for the lukewarm.

This book's for you.
In fact, this book is for all of us, all those who work while the others dine.
For this job of love and nerves and madness,
For this life against the current.
For that fire you never really put out.

And one more for The Rolling Stones and Prince —my gods, my kings, my prophets.
I've lived, burned, and danced to the Glimmer Twins and his Purple Highness.
They carried me through everything.
Don't you dare trash one of their songs—you're fired on the spot.
Yeah, I'm a fan.

I know ♫ *it's only rock 'n' roll—but I like it.*
Yes, a fan indeed, and a hopeless one.
And to all the others—the giants, the geniuses, the ones who make us dance, feel, cry, and smile.
The ones who make rock, soul, funk, and groove.
The ones who made the soundtrack of our lives.
Because music is everywhere in this book.
Can you imagine this book soundtracked by Justin Bieber or Harry Styles?
Come on. Let's be serious.

And finally—for you...
The readers, the guests, and the curious ones who sat through every course.
Thank you.
I didn't want to leave a "polite memory." I wanted to leave a stain, like a spot of sauce.
A scar burnt in, like a grill mark on a rare steak.
If I managed that, then it's mission accomplished.
This book is raw, sometimes brutal, sometimes light, sometimes hard, but never resting. And let's say it—sometimes pathetic. But it's my life, and I loved every moment of it.
Even if I barely breathe through it, there are flashes of pure, wild joy.
When I cook with headphones on, volume cranked, with my heart's playlist in my ears—the one that makes me weep, jump, ache, and soar—
That's fucking bliss.

I wanted to end on grace, and I've got nothing better than this song.

It's not bitter or regretful. It 's a bit sad, but it carries lucidity, honesty and... it s full of hope. Because I also wrote this for the lost ones, the broken ones, and the ones stuck in a hole.
Crushed by the depths of their darkness.
Kids, there's always a way out.
Don't ever give up.
NEVER.
You can always count on something, and don't be afraid to ask for help.
Sometimes it's a job.
A woman, often.
Our kids, too.
It could be a friend or even a dog.

And finally, I wrote this because I was suffocating.
Because it was this—or explode.
Because sometimes, words are all that's left when the knives are down and the shouting stops.
And you've got to keep standing—and smiling.
I've cooked, yelled, loved, and lived—all to music.
But I never lied.
Not once.
Not on a single line.

I know at one point in life you have to do a kind of inventory.
So why not? Let's give it a try...
Was I a good chef? Ask my old crew.
A good husband? I doubt it, but ask my wife.
A good father? Time will tell. Ask my kid.
a great guitarist? Hell, no, despite all my effort.
But through all, I held the line. Till the end.

Even when I was on my knees.

So, if you sweated between the lines,
If you recognized yourself in the pass, in a dining room, or in a kitchen—then it's done.
The job's finished.
Does this book turn your stomach? Doesn't matter. Drink some lukewarm water, pop an enema, and grab the toilet paper.

If it made you laugh, or cry, or even moved you just a little, then do me one favor:
Go to your fridge, grab a pan, throw in a good knob of butter, and cook yourself something nice.
Music as loud as possible.
And raise a glass to us.
To all the times we cooked for you.
You owe us that much, right?
So—cheers.
To you. To us.
At least, if this book did that, it did its job.

Now I'm leaving.
Not far—just away with my tribe, to live and cook at my own rhythm.
To start over somewhere new—with the speakers still blasting rock and food that still kicks you in the gut.

That's it.
The kitchen is closed.
I'm putting away my knives, my shovel, and my bullshit.

The gas is shut.
But before I leave the room, I just want to tell you one last thing:
If you come back tomorrow,
The pass will still be buzzing.
and I'll be there—behind the line.
So you know where to find me.

That's it.
Lights off.

Jukebox

Chef's extra

You thought it was over?
You really thought I'd leave you on a soft, tender note—all good vibes and redemption arcs?
Dream on. Not my style.
I should've stopped at the epilogue, I know.
But hell, even after I put the shovels away, I still had a little butter left in the fridge and a small trowel in my hand.
So—one more shot for the road?
I'm not walking away just like that, without a final riff.

What you're about to read isn't really a chapter.
It's a bonus.
The thing you hear after the last track when you didn't turn off the sound, when you stayed there in the dark, glass in hand.
It is like a hidden track.
You remember? That thing some bands used to stash at the end of albums, the famous track ninety-nine, the one only the real ones heard.
It's exactly that.
It's a relaxed note after the emotional climb of the epilogue.
Or more like, sometimes at the end of the night, when a customer asks to see the chef—I

come out from the kitchen, apron tossed, jacket clean, half a glass of red in hand, and a little rock still burning in my belly.
A prolongation, an after.
A late-night after-service for the insomniacs.
So, this “thing” is a little bit of all that at once.
It’s not a tidy or romantic ending.
It’s a freewheel exit—a way to short-circuit the critics, torch the rules, and burn the labels one last time.
That’s why changed the police.
To change the mood.

So, listen...
Do you want to stop at the epilogue, with a tear in your eye and your heart full?
Do it.
No one’s going to blame you.
But if you’re greedy, if you still have room for one last bite, one little mignardise...
If you’re wondering why there’s no Madonna, no Beatles, and three generations of DJs missing...
Sit down.
Because now,
You’re in the jukebox.

This book—you read it in stereo.
You’ve got my playlist.
And honestly, I don’t know what was harder—writing the damn thing or picking the songs.
Some were locked in from the start.
Four of them. Not one more.

♫ Jumpin' Jack Flash to open. It was non-negotiable.

♫ Let's Go Crazy—Prince.

♫ Waiting (Reprise)—George Michael, for the epilogue.

And ♫ Where the Streets Have No Name—U2. Didn't know where to put it until I realized it belonged exactly where it is now: at the end. Where it was meant to be.

The rest?
A minefield.
A war zone of eliminations, reversals, and painful cuts.
Some tracks I kept even though I hated myself for it—like the two abominations in the Miami chapter: Guns N' Roses and The Who. Yeah, I had to shower after. I know. It's harsh. But honest.
My loves, my grudges, my picks—they're all part of me. It's my taste and still... my fucking book.
And yes, you've got the right to argue, to think others would've fit better. Between us... Go ahead, make your own playlist.
Stick your soundtrack to it; slap your favorite song onto a chapter you like. Rewrite this book with your music, at your tempo, and make it yours somehow.
That way it might hit you deeper, digging something up deep inside.
Because that's what rock is –

You share it; you scream it together.

So here's my dare:
Since you know my name, hit me up on X, Instagram, or Facebook.
Send me your soundtrack.
Tell me what I got wrong, what you'd have played instead, or your comment about this book.
Go ahead—I can take it. I've got thick skin.

Music helped me write. Set the tone, set the pace.
Some songs didn't make it because they were too clean, too soft, or too predictable.
I love Purple Rain, Stairway to Heaven, all that—but when I tried to write with them, everything fell flat.
So I switched.
Rewrote.
Restarted.
Music isn't just a soundtrack to me; it's a crutch that keeps you standing when life's kicking your ass. It carries you through sadness, through hard times. Like a supersonic jet that flips you from melancholy to joy in ten seconds flat.
One minute you're crying, the next you're dancing on the table.
Or the other way around.

It's the best drug in the world.
It's like foie gras for the soul.

So who's in my pantheon?
The gods, obviously:
The Stones.
Prince.
Pink Floyd.
George Michael.
U2.
Bowie.
AC/DC
I wish I'd squeezed in more:
Led Zep.
Noel Gallagher, Oasis.
Stereophonics.
Luther Vandross. Marvin Gaye.
Brel. Aznavour. Sinatra. John Mayer.
Fleetwood Mac. The Eagles, ZZ Top, and Black Crowes.
But hey, even in love, you have to cut ties.

And since I like to tease, let's talk about who I left out on purpose, yes... the omissions... the juicy part.
No rap.
Today's rap? I'm allergic. Impervious. I need an aspirin in one hand and a puke bag in the other.
Since N.W.A., Public Enemy, Ice-T, Ice Cube, Tupac, Snoop, and Dr. Dre, it's been spinning in circles. No inspiration, washed out, drained. Out of gas

No Madonna. Too vulgar.

Yeah, I know; I'm saying that the pot is calling the kettle black.
No Beyoncé, no Taylor Swift, no Katy Perry, no Ed Sheeran—the "stars of the moment."
Come on... Really? You've heard that stuff?
Do I need to add more?

No country. I love Chris Stapleton, but it doesn't fit my kitchen.
No Springsteen. Love the guy—but too American at the core.
No Dylan—too political, too sixties.
No DJs, no electronic crap. The word "music" doesn't belong in that sentence.
No Presley—too kitsch.

And most controversial of all:
No Beatles.
Yeah, I said it.
I respect the talent. I tried but it just doesn't do shit to me. I find it it boring.
And mostly, It's a faith thing.
Stones or Beatles?
Meat or fish?
Cheese or dessert?
I chose.
And sorry to the purists...
Actually, I am not sorry at all.
Fuck the Beatles

My advice: if you're going to listen to the Stones, listen to them live.

Flashpoint, Steel Wheels Tokyo, or the Brussels '73 European Tour—pure fire. All the live LP they released are awesome.

For U2: 360° Tour in L.A. or U2 Go Home—Slane Castle.

Pink Floyd? Pulse (the live album).
David Gilmour: Live in Pompeii 2016—the ultimate version of "Comfortably Numb." ".
Or his latest masterpiece, "Luck and Strange," and the live album that goes with it.

Regarding Prince.
hell, you can listen to everything as far as I am concerned, but live?
SOTT Tour Rotterdam 87,
Lovesexy Tour Dortmund 88,
Parade Tour Detroit 86,
Purple Rain Tour in Syracuse, 1985
And the final gem, probably the best concert he ever played,
Montreux Jazz Festival in 2009.
Two concerts, one right after the other one.
Both different, two vibes, two setlists.
The first one is jazzy and groovy; the second is rawer, more rock, and lyrical.
He covers Santana, Hendrix, and Presley; it's jaw-dropping.
Trust me, you have never listened to or seen anything like this.

Now, do me one last favor.

I've asked you to cook, to toast, to drink, to vent—now I'm begging you to play.
You or your kids should pick up an instrument. Any instrument.
Triangle, bagpipe, xylophone—anything, but the recorder
Not the goddamn recorder.
We ruined too many kids with that crap. It killed a generation of would-be musicians and shredded too many family eardrums.

Me, I picked up the guitar long ago.
My daughter followed.
And that's probably the best thing I've ever passed down to her—the love of music.
It heals you.
It centers you.
It teaches patience, discipline, surrender, and joy.
So play music.
Go to gigs.
Buy records.
Crank up the volume.
And most of all, feel it.
Forget therapy—it's the best cure on earth.
The two most fun things I've ever held in my hands?
Chef's knives and guitars.
I've got six of each.
And I use them every damn day.

Alright I need to wrap it up, because I can talk about music all fucking day long.

And since my chaos needs its anthem, I'll close with Prince.

♫ Computer Blue.

A track that's totally fucked up but brilliant, and that says everything about me.

A Chaotic jam – like my life.
Raw –like this book.
Electric –like a kitchen in the full fire of the service.

So yeah, let's leave it there.
Alright. That's it.
End of the track.
Now it's over.

www.ingramcontent.com/pod-product-compliance
Lightning Source LLC
LaVergne TN
LVHW090555110826
845146LV00001B/130

* 9 7 9 8 9 9 3 1 0 9 5 9 6 *